NO LONGER EXILES

MICHAEL CROMARTIE is a research fellow in Protestant studies and the director of the Evangelical Studies Project at the Ethics and Public Policy Center in Washington, D.C. He is co-editor, with Richard John Neuhaus, of *Piety and Politics: Evangelicals and Fundamentalists Confront the World*, and editor of *Evangelicals and Foreign Policy, Peace Betrayed? Essays on Pacifism and Politics*, and *Gaining Ground: New Approaches to Poverty and Dependency*.

NO LONGER EXILES

THE RELIGIOUS NEW RIGHT IN AMERICAN POLITICS

EDITED BY

MICHAEL CROMARTIE

ETHICS AND PUBLIC POLICY CENTER

Library of Congress Cataloging-in-Publication Data

No longer exiles : the religious new right in American politics / edited by Michael Cromartie.
p.   cm.
Four papers, followed by commentary, originally presented at a conference held in Washington, DC, in November 1990, organized by the Ethics and Public Policy Center.
Includes index.
1. Evangelicalism—United States—History—20th century—Congresses. 2. Fundamentalism—History—Congresses. 3. Conservatism—United States—History—20th century—Congresses. 4. Conservatism—Religious aspects—Christianity—Congresss. 5. United States—Politics and government—1977–1981—Congresses. 6. United States—Politics and government—1981–1989—Congresses. 7. United States—Politics and government—1989–   —Congresses. 8. United States—Church history—20th century—Congresses. I. Cromartie, Michael. II. Ethics and Public Policy Center (Washington, D.C.) III. Title: Religious new right in American politics.
BR1644.5.U6N62   1992   320.5′5′097309048—dc20   92–32546 CIP

ISBN 0–89633–172–5 (cloth : alk. paper)

Distributed by:

National Book Network
4720 Boston Way
Lanham, MD 20706

3 Henrietta Street
London WC2E 8LU England

All Ethics and Public Policy Center books are produced on acid-free paper. The paper used in this publication meets the minimum requirements of American National Standard for Information Sciences—Permanence of Paper for Printed Library Materials, ANSI Z39.48–1984.   ∞ ™

Ethics and Public Policy Center
1015 Fifteenth Street N.W.
Washington, D.C. 20005
(202) 682–1200

Contents

Preface

H EAVE an egg out a Pullman window," H. L. Mencken wrote in 1924, "and you will hit a fundamentalist almost anywhere in the United States today." To the bewilderment of many, this is still true. And if Mencken were living today, he might give his original point a different spin: "Heave an egg out a window anywhere on Capitol Hill, and you will likely hit an evangelical political activist." The time when political involvement by evangelicals and fundamentalists was seen as worldly, or even sinful, activity has passed. Now political celibacy tends to be considered a dereliction of Christian responsibility.

No eggs were hurled but a wide variety of opinions were expressed when, in November 1990 in Washington, D.C., the Ethics and Public Policy Center brought together twenty-five scholars and activists to discuss the future, and the past, of evangelical political involvement and the Religious New Right. The conference participants, who represented numerous disciplines and perspectives, had all written extensively on, or been involved intimately with, the subject of this book.

Following the Second World War, evangelical and fundamentalist Protestants maintained a rather low public profile until the press became curious about former President Jimmy Carter's born-again Baptist faith. A cover of *Newsweek* magazine declared 1976 "The Year of the Evangelical" largely because of President Carter's outspoken personal faith, the popularity of Charles Colson's bestselling book *Born Again*, and the booming growth that was occurring in conservative Protestant churches. Not since the so-called Scopes monkey trial in 1925 had evangelicals and fundamentalists received so much public attention as they did in the late 1970s and early 1980s when they began to become politically involved.

While conservative Protestants had always found plenty to complain about in the wider society, they remained somewhat aloof from politics before the cultural and legal revolutions of the 1960s and 1970s sent shock waves through their communities. They then became engaged in a "defensive offensive," as Nathan Glazer called it, against what they perceived as aggressive secular and liberal forces bent on disrupting their enclaves of traditional religion. The first priority of the Religious New Right was not to promote particular views; rather, it was to make other evangelicals, fundamentalists, and charismatics aware of the need to become involved in public issues that concerned them. This was not an easy task because many had been taught for decades that such activity was irrelevant.

The attempt by evangelicals and fundamentalists to shape domestic and foreign policy according to their own distinctive theological agendas generated impassioned public debate throughout the past decade. And their influence continues to be strong in the nineties: their presence was felt so strongly at the 1992 Republican National Convention that the *Washington Post* reported they had taken the convention "by surprise with their robust appearance, mustering perhaps 300 of the more than 2,000 delegates, all of them full of spirit and impassioned for the cause."

Today there is perhaps even more debate within the evangelical community itself about the meaning, significance, and future of the Religious New Right. Evangelical political philosophers and activists continue to examine how biblically grounded moral norms enter, and influence, a public arena in which those norms are not universally shared.

The four principal contributors to this volume (a historian, a sociologist, and two political scientists) were specifically asked to "assess the past and scout the future" of the Religious New Right —which is also known as the New Religious Right, the New Christian Right, the Evangelical Right, and simply the Religious Right. Each of their essays is followed by a formal response from a distinquished commentator, and also by more informal observations made at the conference by various participants.

I would like to thank Jacqueline Stark and Dan Maclellan of the Ethics and Public Policy Center staff for their editorial advice and timely assistance. Center interns Hunter Boyd and Elizabeth Lake provided invaluable help with conference arrangements.

We hope that this book will encourage constructive and critical thinking within the American evangelical community and among the wider religious and political communities concerned with the issues addressed here.

MICHAEL CROMARTIE

1

The Religious Right:
A Historical Overview

George Marsden

I F history has laws, the first should be that we cannot predict very much of it. Who in the 1950s would have predicted the upheavals of the 1960s? At the end of the 1960s, pundits were charting a new age of Aquarius; what they ended up with was the age of Ronald Reagan. Or who in 1975 predicted the flourishing of the Religious Right in American politics? Theories of secularization told us that conservative religion would go away.

It is hazardous, then, to predict what will happen to the Religious Right. The best a historian can offer is some understanding of how religiously motivated politics fits into the larger patterns of American history and some speculations on what may be different about the future.

Many observers assume that the entry of outspoken religious

George Marsden is the Francis A. McAnaney Professor of History at the University of Notre Dame. He was formerly professor of American religious history at Duke University Divinity School and at Calvin College. His numerous books include *Fundamentalism and American Culture* and *Reforming Fundamentalism: Fuller Seminary and the New Evangelicalism*. The first two-thirds of this paper is adapted from "Afterword: Religion, Politics, and the Search for an American Consensus," in *Religion and American Politics: From the Colonial Period to the 1980s*, ed. Mark A. Noll (New York: Oxford University Press, 1989).

conservatives into American politics is a departure from custom. In fact, for better or for worse, religion has always been an element of the American political heritage. Therefore, the resurgence of the Religious Right should actually be seen as a revival of one of the nation's major political traditions.

In the American colonial era it was taken for granted that religion and politics were linked. There were established churches in Western nations, and religion was often integral to national identity. Throughout the period a central political theme was the cold war between Protestants and Catholics. The British colonies were Protestant outposts in a predominately Catholic atmosphere. The deep rivalry between these two churches dominated American thought, much as the Cold War between Marxists and non-Marxists nations dominated world politics for decades after World War II.

Moreover, if anti-Catholicism constituted a major foreign-policy issue, the rivalry between Anglicans and Calvinists was a primary theme in colonial domestic struggles. The heirs to Puritanism in New England shared with the Scotch-Irish Presbyterians of the middle colonies and inland southern settlements a particularly militant opposition to the establishment of Anglicanism as a state-supported religion throughout the colonies. According to their purist views, Anglicanism was only a step away from Catholicism and tyranny. Baptists had long held similar views.

Eighteenth-century English dissenters (non-Anglicans) developed a major political movement around their critique of the privileges of royal and ecclesiastical power. This "Real Whig" outlook drew on the traditional Puritan opposition to the Anglican crown, formulating principles of liberty and justice that became commonplace among American revolutionaries. These principles, as articulated in the language of the Enlightenment, asserted self-evident truths of morality. Enlightened Americans who might, like Thomas Jefferson, be Anglicans by birth could readily adopt such principles, including the opposition to the political establishment of privilege for a particular church.

The Constitution of 1787 defined the new nation in secular terms. Though this stemmed in part from the anti-establishment sentiments of some of the founders, it reflected just as much a high regard for religion in American life. As John F. Wilson has suggested, religion's scant appearance in the Constitution was a reflection not of its insignificance, but rather of its abundant importance. Had the Constitution taken a stand on the divisive religious issues of the day, its chances of ratification would have been slim.[1] The First Amendment articulated the hands-off policy. It ensured that there would be no federal establishment and that the federal government would not interfere with the free exercise of religion. The intent of the Framers was clearly to constrain the federal government from interfering even with the state establishment of religion, and in fact such establishment continued in New England for decades after the new nation was founded.

Early American Attitudes Toward Politics and Religion

Out of the American revolutionary experience, and the unsettled questions left by the Constitution, two distinct attitudes toward politics and religion developed. On one side stood those in the Jeffersonian tradition who saw religion as tribal and divisive. They noted how ethnic and regional rivalries were heightened by religious conflicts that threatened national unity. Government, in their view, must distance itself from direct religious interests. For them, the acceptance of diversity became a particularly important moral duty. This approach was supported by Baptists and others seeking to protect the churches from the state.

On the other side stood people, particularly citizens of New England, who saw a more positive role for Christianity in national life. Though they, too, feared tribal diversity, they were intent on uniting the nation under divinely sanctioned moral principles. Like their Puritan forebears, they believed the Bible was an important guide for national righteousness. In their reading of the Real Whig tradition, religious hierarchy and political authoritarianism went hand in hand. Thus on one side of the ledger lay Catholicism, Anglicanism, centralized monarchical power, corruption, and tyranny; on the other, Protestantism, Puritanism, representative government, virtue, and freedom.

In the early nineteenth century an evangelical version of this outlook emerged, with strong roots in New England and Puritanism. The Great Awakening of the eighteenth century had provided a bridge between Puritanism and democratic revolution. This Second Great Awakening, continuing throughout the first half of the century and longer, expanded the influence of revivalist or evangelical Protestantism. Especially in the North, this movement furnished the religious rationale for a cultural outlook that became a central and long-lasting element of American political life.

Its adherents were usually of English descent and religiously evangelical, although there were some Unitarians among them. Culturally aggressive New England Yankees provided the leadership. Reflecting their Puritan heritage, they sought the conversion of individuals, and strongly favored applying Christian principles to the transformation of society. This would be accomplished by those converted individuals as they cultivated the virtues of industry, thrift, and personal purity, and by voluntary societies of such individuals, banding together for religious, educational, and political causes.

One of the early political expressions of this impulse was the formation of the Anti-Mason party. Outside this Puritan evangelical context, the party would have seemed anomalous in American political history. The secret order of the Masons appeared to these evangelicals as an ominous false religion, one that appealed especially to freethinkers. In 1828 Anti-Masons were numerous enough to deliver nearly half of New York's electoral votes to John Quincy Adams. Merging with the new Whig party, they became the base for the party's important "conscience" wing, counting among their numbers such strong proponents of anti-slavery as Thaddeus Stevens and William H. Seward. Evangelist Charles Finney was an ardent Anti-Mason. (After the Civil War, when the anti-slavery issue was settled, Finney returned to the unfinished business of Anti-Masonism, allying himself with Jonathan Blanchard, president of Wheaton College in Illinois. Under Blanchard's son Charles, Wheaton became a direct link to twentieth-century fundamentalism). The Whig party of the 1830s and 1840s included a substantial New England element, which continued the effort to regulate society according to evangelical principles,[2] but the drive took on a new shape with the party's demise.

The Catholic Factor

The new factor in the equation was the rise of Catholic political power. Before the mid-nineteenth century the American rivalries had been intra-Protestant. Scotch-Irish Protestants had been pivotal in American politics through the nation's first half century. Disliking the New Englanders and their schemes for moral regulation, they had allied themselves with the South, which had dominated the politics of the early era. By the 1850s, however, with the influx of Catholics to the Democratic party, the picture changed. Catholics who, like the Scotch-Irish, objected to the Yankee ideal of a monolithic Protestant moral commonwealth, swelled the ranks of the Democrats. But the Scotch-Irish, despising the Catholics even more than they disliked the New Englanders, left the Democratic fold, along with some Baptists and Methodists. As the historian Robert Kelley observes, whereas previously the party of culturally aggressive Protestantism had been *English*, now it was a *British* lineup against the detested Irish Catholics.[3]

Explicit anti-Catholicism emerged as the major political issue of the 1850s. In 1856 the anti-Catholic, nativist Know-Nothing party won 21 per cent of the popular vote for its presidential candidate, Millard Fillmore. Following his defeat, the party merged with the anti-slavery and purely regional Republican party. The result was a Republican party with a strong Puritan-evangelical component, bent on regulating society according to Christian principles. Anti-slavery was the greatest achievement of this outlook, but anti-Catholicism and opposition to alcohol were just as distinguishing features.

This party fostered an insider-versus-outsider attitude toward America and Americanism. Ethnically, it was predominately British; economically, it was thoroughly allied with the dominant business community. Both these features reinforced its insider view of itself. The Puritan-Methodist ethic of self-help, moral discipline, and social responsibility, prevalent in American education, defined its version of Americanism.

In the meantime, the post-1840 Democratic party was increasingly the party of outsiders. Its largest components were Catholics and Southerners, two groups with almost nothing in common but a disdain for Republicans and their self-righteous evangelical desire to impose their version of Christian morality on the nation.

Northern evangelicals—Congregationalists, New School Presbyterians, most Methodists, and most Baptists—usually voted Republican. High Church, liturgical, and confessional Protestants (including some German Lutherans), all of whom had reservations about the evangelical-Puritan version of Christian America, were more likely to vote Democratic. So, too, were important groups of evangelical Protestants who were, in the tradition of Roger Williams, sufficiently sectarian to question the possibility of establishing a Christian political order.[4]

Though by the late nineteenth century the Republican party had become a pragmatic coalition and could no longer be described as an evangelical voluntary society writ large, it nevertheless retained its fervor for building a Protestant Christian moral consensus. In a notorious incident during the 1884 presidential campaign, a supporter of Republican James G. Blaine said that a vote for Cleveland was a vote for "rum, Romanism, and rebellion." Blaine ultimately repudiated the statement, but too late, and it probably cost him the election. It is revealing that at this late date Republicans were still appealing to nativism, but more importantly, its negative impact on their campaign signaled the end of the era, begun with the Anti-Mason movement, in which evangelical Protestantism had been an explicitly partisan factor in American political life. Although Prohibition remained a critical issue for the evangelicals for another half century, neither party could afford to remain as overtly sectarian as it had been. Indeed, they were closely enough matched that Republicans found themselves cultivating some Catholic support while Democrats courted some evangelicals. After a period in which religion had largely worked against national consensus, this constituted major change.

Away From Exclusion

A turning point in the reorientation of American politics came in 1896, when the Democrats ran the evangelical William Jennings Bryan for president. By the time Bryan had run twice more, in

1900 and 1908, the Democratic party had incorporated an interventionist, reformist element, much like that of the Republican party, and was even evincing strong support for the arch-evangelical cause of Prohibition.[5] Democrats ended their progressive era by electing Woodrow Wilson. Though a Southerner, the Presbyterian Wilson was as Puritan as any New Englander who ever held office.

Just as important, however, was what was happening to the Republicans. The party of McKinley and Mark Hanna had toned down its evangelical image and attracted some Catholics, though it was still an overwhelmingly Protestant party with strong assimilationists goals. It represented a centripetal force in America attempting to counter centrifugal tendencies accentuated by immigration. Public education became sacrosanct, providing a means for teaching immigrants American virtues. The social gospel of the Republicans remained a program for Christianizing America, but they had suppressed its old, exclusivist evangelical Protestant elements in order to absorb the new immigrants into their domain.

In effect, the liberalized Protestantism and the somewhat secularized social reform of this progressive era allowed the heirs to accomplish once again what their more explicitly evangelical forebears had achieved in the 1860s: Northern Protestant dominance. As Robert Kelley puts it, the party patterns set in the progressive era, from 1894 to 1930, coincided with "the years of Northern WASP ascendancy in all things, including government, literature, scholarship, the arts, and the economy."[6]

Here we see an instance of an American pattern of secularization pointed out long ago by Martin Marty. Secularization took place not through a developing hostility between religion and the dominant culture, but by a blending of their goals. Republican-Protestant hegemony no longer had to be explicitly Protestant. It now simply represented a certain concept of civilization that, though still equivalent in most Republicans' minds to Christian civilization, could be advanced by progressive reform principles of morality that people from all traditions might share. Many Democrats of this era, represented by Bryan and Wilson, adopted this slightly secularized Protestant vision as thoroughly as the Republicans did. The great missionary enthusiasm that swept through the nation's colleges grew out of the impulse to help the world by advancing Christian civilization. Wilson's secularized post-millennial vision of the American mission—to make the world safe for democracy—reflected a similar outlook. Religion, in short, had begun to move the nation toward consensus.

Yet despite this softening of the Protestant hegemony into a melting-pot ideal of citizenship, democracy, and values taught to all in the public schools, the realignment of 1896 did not entirely disrupt the older party patterns.[7] As late as the election of 1960, the Democratic party's strongest bases remained the old South and Catholic communities, while old-line Protestants still tended to be disproportionately Republican. With the coming of the Depression and the New Deal, however, economic issues dominated party politics, and except when the Democrats ran Catholic candidates in 1928 and 1960, explicit religion was relegated to a ceremonial role.

Although many politicians were Catholics during this era, almost none could be called Catholic politicians in the sense that they were applying Catholic principles to politics. Rather, Catholic politicians were Americanizing. And the price of being an American politician for a Catholic was to leave substantive Catholicism at the church door. Al Smith, when asked by a reporter about the Pope's latest encyclical, replied, "What the hell is an encyclical?"[8] Catholics had learned to play the twentieth-century game of appealing to the nation's religious heritage, but in a purely ceremonial way. John F. Kennedy, as Robert Bellah noted in a classic essay, was particularly adept at using the symbols of American civil religion.[9]

Following the progressive era, religion played a substantive role in American politics only through the civil-rights movement. Blacks—whose political style had been set by mid-nineteenth-century Republican models, and for whom the clergy were traditional community spokespersons in the pattern of Puritan New England—could still challenge the collective conscience of the nation.

The Ideal of Secularized Consensus

The wider pattern, from 1896 to about 1968, was a growing ideal of secularized consensus. Despite the persisting ethno-religious patterns, some differences on economic policy, and varying degrees of cold warriorism, the two parties were now much alike. With some significant exceptions, it was difficult to find any real differences in principle between them. Indeed, the genius of American politics seemed to be that the two parties did not stand for much of anything. George Wallace's campaign slogan of 1968, that there was not "a dime's worth of difference" between the two parties, seemed accurate. Supporters of Eugene McCarthy could agree.

Martin Marty has referred to a "four-faith" pluralism that emerged in consensus America during the 1950s. And Will Herberg showed in 1955 that although Protestants, Catholics, and Jews had differing formal religions, they had much in common in the operative religion of faith in the American way of life.[10] Marty's fourth faith, secularism, was acceptable as a private option and still fit within the consensus.[11]

From our retrospective vantage point, it is striking that this accurate portrayal of American public life in the consensus era omits any role for explicitly evangelical Protestantism.

As mainline Protestants had blended into the secularized consensus, fundamentalists, conservative Protestants, or explicit "evangelicals" had been forced out. Although during the 1920s they had gained some national prominence in anti-evolution campaigns and in opposition to Al Smith, they had soon faded as a serious political force. During the next forty years, from 1928 to 1968, there were always right-wing evangelists trying to rally support on political issues, but most evangelicals remained on the fringes of American politics. Either they lapsed into political inactivity, or they blended in with conservative Republicans in the North or as birthright Democrats in the South. But in their separation, it is important to note, evangelicals were beginning to nurture a dissidence that would one day threaten the consensus. They were dissenting, not only from the liberal theology that made the consensus possible, but also from some of the progressive social policies that grew out of the social gospel.

By 1968 the liberal New Deal consensus had broken down. The Vietnam War, the rioting of blacks, and the counterculture had destroyed the illusion of a liberal-Protestant-Catholic-Jewish-secu-

lar-good-citizenship concord. While progressives tried to rebuild
an even more secular, inclusive, and pluralistic consensus, conservatives sharply disagreed. Capitalizing at first on what seemed a
largely secular backlash, they mobilized around anti-Communism
and love-it-or-leave-it Americanism. Following the Vietnam War
and the presidency of Richard Nixon, a new, more religious
movement began to coalesce around ethical issues such as abortion,
pornography, and the Equal Rights Amendment, and symbolic
religious issues such as school prayer.

The Rise of the Religious Right

After 1976 it was increasingly clear that a substantial evangelical,
fundamentalist, and Pentecostal-charismatic constituency could be
mobilized around these issues. Only a portion of theologically
conservative evangelicals, however, adopted this stance on the political right. The evangelical movement itself was a divided coalition,
maintaining at best a tenuous anti-liberal theological unity among
a myriad of subgroups and denominations. Although a solid contingent of evangelicals could be organized, in the Moral Majority,
for example, or for the Pat Robertson campaign of 1988, evangelicalism was far from unified as a political force.

Nevertheless, those who did mobilize had a significant effect on
the patterns of American political life. In addition to increasing the
number of those on the Republican right, they helped supply a
rhetoric with which the party generally could reclaim some still-
potent symbols from its nineteenth-century heritage. Strikingly
absent, however, was anti-Catholicism. Protestant evangelicals and
conservative Catholics (as well as Mormons and members of the
Unification Church) now made common cause on anti-Communism and family issues. Such remarkable alliances suggested that,
despite the explicitly evangelical stance of its leadership, the Religious Right was forming a political consensus in which the exclu-
siveness of evangelicalism would be toned down. At the same time,
the movement drew in the natural Anglo-Protestant evangelical
constituency of the South, which adopted the revivified Christian
America ideal with particular fervor. Though not overtly racist, the
new coalition forsook its nineteenth-century heritage of advocating
the black cause.

As was true for evangelical Republicans in the era of Ulysses S. Grant, what conservatives actually got with the victory of Ronald Reagan fell far short of the Christian America of their rhetoric. In this second Gilded Age, as in the first, the mixture of high moral aspirations of Christian civilization with the pragmatic, individualistic acquisitiveness of business interests inevitably compromised the ideal.

Despite the anomalies, an important element of the American political heritage had been revived. Nineteenth-century Anti-Masonism and the contemporary war on secular humanism are generically related, even if the center of gravity has moved south. In the face of growing pluralism and moral inclusivism, which became increasingly the trademarks of the Democratic party, one significant wing of Republicanism recovered the ideals of building a coalition around a militant, broadly Christian, anti-secularist, and anti-Communist heritage. This view of the essence of what it means to be an American conflicts sharply with a more inclusivist moral vision.

Religious Right Achievements

It might be objected that the long history of Christianity and American politics has little relevance to the recent rise of the Religious Right.[12] After all, conditions in the United States today are much different from those of the nineteenth century, and many of the specific issues raised by the Religious Right are new.

I think, however, that we can see the continuities, as well as some discontinuities, by recognizing the achievements of the Religious Right on three distinguishable levels.

The first of these levels is the symbolic or the rhetorical. Here the historical heritage has a great deal of relevance. Many of the current symbols of American politics, such as prayer, purity, family, and flag, are deeply rooted in the American past. Some argue that the Religious Right contributed little to this symbolic revival, and simply rode the coattails of Ronald Reagan, the master of the symbolic politics of nostalgia. It is true that as Reagan's presidency wore on, it became apparent to the leadership of the Religious Right that his commitment to their cause lacked substance. George Bush, who in 1988 also successfully used the revived symbols, was even less committed. The symbols might thus be seen as the creation of political marketing. But because the presidents' coalitions included conspicuous Religious Right constituents who both took the rhetoric seriously and were using it for substantive proposals and programs, it has gained a plausibility it might not have had otherwise. It was not *simply* advertising, for it pointed to actual possibilities.

At the second level, the Religious Right has revived serious moral issues as substantive topics for the American political agenda. Again, many of these, like standards for family and decency, the support of free enterprise against socialism, and prayer in the public schools, are directly rooted in the nineteenth century. Other issues, such as anti-abortion (at least for Protestants) were relatively new, while a number of older issues, among them temperance and Sabbatarianism, have disappeared. But a more important issue linking the concerns of the Religious Right with the longer tradition of Christianity in American politics is the belief that God's law, as understood in conservative readings of Scripture,[13] ought to be normative in determining the laws of the nation. A few decades ago, most political analysts thought that approach was as dead as the divine right of kings. That the Religious Right had managed to raise these concerns in the American political setting of the late twentieth century is a remarkable achievement. It is an achievement made possible only by a long-held American tradition of applying the Bible to politics. Even when such issues were absent from America's secularized political discussion, they were preserved for many in their religious organizations, and hence could be revived as serious concerns.

The third level of the Religious Right's impact is that of political organization and influence on actual policy. Here the achievement has been more limited. Nonetheless, there have been a few gains in checking permissiveness and some successful consciousness-raising, supported by conservative court appointments, regarding such issues as discrimination against conservative religion in public life, especially education and abortion. Even here, it is not hard to find substantial continuity with the past.

Back to the Future

How, then, do these continuities with the past relate to our understanding of the future of the Religious Right in American politics? I can think of five points.

1. Christianity in American politics has a very long history and is not likely to disappear entirely. This long tradition of mixing religion and politics helps account for the ability of conservative religious leaders in the 1980s to re-enter the political mainstream. What happened in the 1980s was not an aberration. Given the right degree of cultural crisis, as we had in the post–World War I era and the post-Vietnam era, religious and cultural fundamentalists can appeal to parts of the American tradition that are historically rooted.

2. On the other hand, it seems unlikely that religiously generated political programs can *sustain* their impact on the political mainstream for an extended time. In the twentieth century they have risen to the surface only in the 1920s and the 1980s. More typically, politically oriented religious conservatives—like Carl McIntire, Billy James Hargis, and Edgar C. Bundy in the 1950s, or Father Coughlin and Gerald B. Winrod in the 1930s—have been there, loudly calling for action, but have found little hearing in the mainstream.

In fact, it appears that the recent cycle of national prominence has passed its peak. The scandals that rocked the television evangelists at the end of the 1980s damaged their collective credibility, and, as Pat Robertson found out when a few of his exaggerations were exposed, provided opportunities to dismiss them as a serious political force. Given the cyclical nature of their political roles in the twentieth century, they are unlikely to recover quickly, once their momentum has receded.

3. Perhaps, though, the largest problem for the religious-political right, if it is to recover, is to find a unified voice. American evangelicalism has provided much of the leadership for an organized political movement but is itself extremely diverse. It is not one movement but many, united by some common religious beliefs. Even in its prime, in the nineteenth century, it was sharply divided

on many issues, and disastrously so on slavery. Today many evangelicals shun the political far right; Jimmy Carter and Mark Hatfield provide good examples. Although it is easy to say that traditional Judeo-Christian moral values should shape American politics, it is difficult to agree on *which* values, and on what means Christians should use to promote them.

Even among politically conservative evangelicals, there are important divisions. Most evangelicals, for example, did not vote for Pat Robertson. Jerry Falwell, who as a fundamentalist may have been uneasy about Robertson as a charismatic, supported Bush. The alliance with the Catholic political right is the most important countervailing force but does not resolve the problem of diversity within the movement.

Moreover, within most of the major conservative evangelical groups, there is a deep ambivalence about whether Christians should organize politically. Conservative Southern Baptists, who often sound like the leading champions of the Puritan ambition to make God's law the law of the land, also claim the tradition of Roger Williams and the separation of church and state. Fundamentalists, Pentecostals, and charismatics share this ambivalence. Many of them are dispensational pre-millennialists who regard the civilizations of the current "dispensation" as condemned. Consistent dispensationalists have proclaimed that adopting political programs is like cleaning the staterooms on the Titanic after it has hit the iceberg. In their view, it is far more important simply to preach the Gospel and to rescue souls for the next life. Jerry Falwell's retreat to caring for his local church draws on this tradition of putting evangelism first.

4. The most plausible scenario for the Religious Right in the 1990s is that it will be more fragmented, localized, and oriented toward single issues than it was in the 1980s.[14]

It is quite possible that much the same thing will happen to the New Right of the 1980s as happened to the New Left of the 1960s. I recall hearing anti-war activist Daniel Berrigan speak around 1975 in a large auditorium where a crowd of two hundred looked meager. He lamented that since the end of the war the movement had fragmented into sub-causes.

The analogy may be instructive. Disunity and disappearance from the national headlines are far different from defeat. Much of the New Left agenda, in moderated form, has become a permanent fixture of the national agenda. The Religious Right may have succeeded in establishing itself as a player in American politics that cannot be dismissed. It has raised a set of moral concerns that are likely to slow movement toward a totally permissive society.

What happened to the fundamentalism of the 1920s may be equally instructive. Having lost its national prominence, it reorganized, built new institutions, and flourished at the local level. It also divided into a separatist hard-liner party and a more moderate wing, which re-emerged as nationally prominent under the leadership of Billy Graham. Perhaps the political fundamentalism of the 1980s, like the old fundamentalism of the 1920s and the New Left of the 1960s, will have its longest-lasting impact in a more moderate guise.

5. Moderation, or at least flexibility, is necessary to deal with one major limitation on the ability of the Religious Right to influence the American future. At present, the narrow ethnic base of the movement diminishes the likelihood that the specifics of its agenda will be largely and lastingly implemented. Predominantly Northern European, the base has been strengthed by the reunion of South and North. Some Catholic conservatives add variety to the coalition. But the movement has not made major inroads into the increasingly important African-American and Hispanic communities. Among African-Americans, for instance, there are many evangelical Bible believers who could be enlisted to support aspects of a traditionalist moral agenda. For this to happen, however, the Religious Right will have to be flexible enough to abandon or modify some of its positions on economic issues. Though they are proclaimed as God's will, they are widely perceived to be the sanctified self-interest of a social group with a long record of racism. Repudiating racism, as most of the leadership has done, is an important first step. Yet if it cannot demonstrate greater concern for racial and ethnic minorities, or enlist their support, leadership, and perspectives, the Religious Right is unlikely to gain wide enough credibility for its political agenda to be long sustained.

It is doubtful, however, that the Religious Right will become flexible or moderate enough to build such a coalition. It is more likely that if increasing numbers of Americans share the Religious Right's desire to bring Christianity and normative moral concerns back into the American political agenda, there will be increasing disunity among their numbers.

Perhaps the most serious problems facing the Religious Right is a theoretical one. It is one thing to try to relate Christianity, even traditional or biblical Christianity, to politics. It is quite another to try to relate such concerns to specific political policies. Those who see the relationship of their Christianity to their politics as simple must be extraordinarily dogmatic. Such dogmatism is not likely to be the basis of a large or lasting political coalition, especially in a nation as diverse in traditions as America.

But by now I appear to have forgotten history's first law. Historians who try to serve as prophets know enough to realize that within the next five years there will probably be a dramatic change that no one anticipated, and all bets, or at least most bets, will be off. We can learn from the patterns of the past something of the range of possibilities for the future. After that, however, it is anybody's guess.

Response

Grant Wacker

MARSDEN'S argument can be broken into three parts. The first is that a strong Whig-Republican movement, or what might be called a "Conscience Coalition," emerged in the United States in the first quarter of the nineteenth century and dominated public discourse through the first quarter of the twentieth century. As an enduring expression of the social and cultural interests of white anglo male Protestants (WAMPs), that coalition distinguished itself in a number of ways. The most important was its perennial desire to intervene in American culture in order to uphold biblical—or at least what it regarded as biblical—standards of private and public morality.

The second part of Marsden's argument is that in the last decades of the nineteenth century, the old Conscience Coalition was gradually displaced by a quite different one, which he calls the "four-faith consensus." Those four faiths were Protestantism, Catholicism, Judaism, and secularism. Though oriented toward the concerns of small business, the four-faith consensus proved increasingly sympathetic to the reform goals of the Square Deal, the New Deal, and the Fair Deal. Like the Conscience Coalition, it generally represented the values of the dominant middle class. The main difference between the old Conscience Coalition and the new four-faith consensus was that the latter offered little place for the ideals of conservative Christians. Thus in the late 1960s the four-faith consensus provoked an adversarial movement commonly called the "Evangelical Right."

This leads to the third and most important feature of Marsden's argument: the Evangelical Right of the 1970s and 1980s repre-

Grant Wacker is an associate professor of history of religion in America at the Duke University Divinity School. He has published numerous essays in scholarly journals and magazines.

sented a rebirth if not a continuation, of the Conscience Coalition of the nineteenth century. Of course there were major differences, but on the whole the Evangelical Right displayed little interest in economic redistribution and favored intervention in the private and public lives of the citizenry in the interests of biblical morality. Marsden states the point carefully, yet unequivocally: the Evangelical Right "helped supply a rhetoric with which the [Republican] party generally could reclaim some still-potent symbols from its nineteenth-century heritage."

Marsden's argument is cogent.[1] The old Conscience Coalition and the new Evangelical Right undeniably bear a strong family resemblance. Both are predominantly populated by conservative Protestants, and both believe it would be a good thing if the rest of the world were too. Both evince an almost instinctive propensity to blame their troubles upon outside conspirators. Both display considerable—some would say astonishing—pragmatism. The Conscience Coalition happily worked with Unitarians and free-thinkers to achieve its political goals, and the Evangelical Right just as readily consorts with Jews and Mormons for the same reasons.

Nonetheless, family resemblance is one thing, genetic historical linkage is quite another. Social phenomena widely separated in time and space may look like one another, but that does not make them heirs of a single tradition. Although sixteenth-century Mennonites were dead ringer's for seventeenth-century Quakers, the actual historical connections between them were few and far between. Therefore the question is this: was the old Conscience Coalition, as Marsden suggests, the biological parent of the new Evangelical Right? If it was, we should be able to see a continual— if not continuous—line of connection running from the nineteenth to the late twentieth century. We should be able to see how networks of persons, working together in definable institutional channels, mediated the tradition from Point A to Point B. But do we?

Possible Links

One possible carrier was one or both of the major political parties. Upon scrutiny, however, the Republican party does not prove a strong candidate for that role, partly because many in the old Conscience Coalition were Democrats. It is difficult to imagine anyone more driven by the elusive whisperings of conscience than a William Jennings Bryan or a Woodrow Wilson—or, for that matter, a Jimmy Carter. And as Booth Fowler's essay in this volume demonstrates, while most politically conservative evangelicals today are aligned with the Republican party, the Republican party hardly is aligned with the Evangelical Right. Despite an occasional round of golf with Billy Graham, the high command of the Republican party has shown itself stubbornly uninterested in the fundamental concerns of the Evangelical Right. The Democratic party works even less well in the carrier role. Its nineteenth-century record on "conscience" issues was spotty, and its current attitude toward the Evangelical Right is wary at best, contemptuous at worst.

Is it possible that the institutional carrier linking the old Conscience Coalition with the new Evangelical Right was one or more of the major Protestant denominations? Not likely. The Conscience Coalition found its primary denominational base among Congregationalists, Episcopalians, northern Presbyterians, and, to a lesser extent, northern Methodists and Baptists. Today the leaders of those denominations tend to avoid the agenda of the Evangelical Right, and many actually seek to undermine it. The Evangelical Right finds its main denominational support among Pentecostals, independent fundamentalists, and Mormons. Admittedly, the sprawling Southern Baptist Convention complicates the issue. In the nineteenth century it upheld some of the ideals of the Conscience Coalition (such as temperance) but not others (such as black rights). While it is true that the current leadership espouses the Evangelical Right's agenda, there is ample evidence that the leadership represents only a minority—albeit a large minority—of the grassroots Southern Baptist constituency.[2] All together, then, the denominational story seems too tangled to offer a clear line of tradition.

What about popular religious periodicals? Did they transmit the cultural concerns of conservative Protestants from the late nineteenth to the late twentieth century? Again, probably not. Most of the organs that exemplified the values of the Conscience Coalition failed to survive much past the turn of the century. One thinks of

—and laments—the passing of one-time giants such as the *Outlook*, the *Independent*, and the *Record of Christian Work*. The few periodicals that did survive seem to have done so either by secularizing or by redefining their aims. The evolution of the happily inspirational *Godey's Lady's Book* to the antiseptically non-religious *Ladies' Home Journal* illustrates the first point. The evolution of *Bibliotheca Sacra* from an organ of mainline Protestant scholarship to a voice of sectarian fundamentalism illustrates the second. Although some periodicals associated with the Evangelical Right, such as *Moody Monthly*, can trace their origins to the cultural milieu of the Conscience Coalition, most, such as *Christianity Today* and *Charisma*, are products of post–World War II evangelical stirrings.

Do we find the requisite links in structural factors such as regional identity or in social class? The provenance of the old Conscience Coalition was Northern and, to a lesser extent, urban. The strength of the Evangelical Right lies in the Sun Belt. The different class constituencies of the two movements offer a still sharper contrast. The leaders of the Conscience Coalition indisputably walked the corridors of the secular and religious power establishment. Consider the case of the noted conservative Baptist theologian Augustus H. Strong. The extended Strong family included the well-known liberal theologian Josiah Strong, prominent banker Benjamin Strong, mining engineer and financier Charles Lyman Strong, navy admiral James Hooker Strong, Northfield College president John Woodward Strong, Wisconsin lawyer and legislator Moses McClure Strong, Topeka and Santa Fe Railroad president William Barstrow Strong, and New York City mayor and Supreme Court justice William L. Strong.[3] The point here is that leaders of the Conscience Coalition were not simply an elite, men with power, but members of a hereditary social establishment, men born to privilege.

Do we see similar trappings of secular power and privilege among the leaders of the Evangelical Right? Perhaps a few. Missouri governor John Ashcroft, an active Assemblies of God layman, is a graduate of Yale College and the University of Chicago Law School. Onetime presidential candidate Pat Robertson is the son of a United States senator and a graduate of Washington and Lee and the Yale Law School. Yet they are the exceptions that prove the rule.

Ashcroft's father served as the president of a small Pentecostal college in Missouri. As for Robertson, it is significant that after his conversion he sought theological training not at Yale Divinity School, but at the sectarian, if not fundamentalist, New York Theological Seminary. Indeed, he usually is treated in the establishment press more as an object of polite condescension than as a pundit with something important to say.

Can it be claimed that the two movements were bonded by an unbroken continuity of cultural concerns? Although it would be preposterous to suggest that the aims of the Conscience Coalition and the Evangelical Right were wholly different, it is important to note how many of the issues dear to the hearts of the former fail to exercise the latter, and vice versa. The Conscience Coalition saw alcohol as the most dire social problem of the age. It was deeply troubled by the growth of non-Anglo immigration in general and by the growth of the Roman Catholic Church in particular. Other worries included tariffs, monetary standards, municipal reform, the power of conglomerates, and Spanish imperialism.

The Evangelical Right, on the other hand, pays lip service to temperance but clearly regards Prohibition as a lost cause. It ignores immigration and happily accepts support from the Roman Catholic Church whenever the Church is willing to give it. Monetary reform and conglomerate-busting rarely poke above the horizon of consciousness. Drugs may be the modern equivalent of alcohol, and red-white-and-blue patriotism aimed against Iraq or the People's Republic of China may be the modern equivalent of anti-Spanish sentiment. But functional equivalences do not equal a living tradition. What the Evangelical Right *is* concerned about is the proper role of women, the discipline and education of children, and what historian Peter Kaufman has aptly called "south of the belt" issues: abortion, homosexuality, and non-marital sex. It is possible that the goals of the Conscience Coalition would have been the goals of the Evangelical Right if the world of the 1890s had been the world of the 1990s. But it was not. And the principled pacifism of a William Jennings Bryan shows that it is more than a little risky to assume that conservative Protestants of the past would have behaved exactly like conservative Protestants of the present.

Certain educational institutions might offer the best possibility for a continuous link between the Conscience Coalition and the Evangelical Right. The strongest candidate is Wheaton College in Illinois. The similarity between Jonathan Blanchard and Billy Graham suggests that occasionally time really does stand still. Several other institutions spring to mind. Gordon College, David Lipscomb College, Moody Bible Institute, perhaps Southern Baptist Seminary, among others, bridge the eras and movements. Still, the real bastions of the Evangelical Right—Oral Roberts University, Regent University, Liberty Baptist University, Criswell School of Theology—are so new they do not need to worry about building library buildings; all they require, someone has quipped, is cellophane packets for the microfiche.

Significant Differences

Where, then, does that leave us? While the Conscience Coalition and the Evangelical Right undeniably bear a strong family resemblance, it is not at all clear that the former directly fathered the latter. On the whole we do better to focus on the differences that separated the two eras and the two movements. Beside the fact that differences are usually more interesting anyway, in this instance the differences seem to offer a richer harvest of explanatory possibilities. To take a case in point, in *Defenders of God: The Fundamentalist Revolt Against the Modern Age* (1989), Duke University religion professor Bruce Lawrence persuasively argued that the technological and cultural changes that came about after the First World War created a climate substantially, perhaps radically, different from the world of the previous generation. Technologically, the twentieth century witnessed the ability of a power elite to manipulate the channels of communication to an extent and in a manner that was unimaginable in times past. Culturally, the twentieth century introduced non-theism as the only acceptable mode of public discourse, along with the assumption that the secular nation-state rightfully stood as the final arbiter of all questions of value. If Lawrence is correct, it is against *that* backdrop—the backdrop posed by the peculiarly twentieth-century absolutes of amoral technology and secular nationalism—that the rise of the Evangelical Right must be understood.

As historians, we are committed to the task of tracing roots as far back as possible. That professional inclination readily connects with the Evangelical Right's own powerful desire to excavate a usable past for itself. The colonial (more precisely, Norman Rockwell colonial) architecture of Pat Robertson's Regent University is evidence enough of that. But sometimes the more difficult task is to discern not only where the roots lead but where they do not. This time, I suspect, the search does not take us back to the late nineteenth century and the reforming zeal of the Women's Christian Temperance Union or the Northfield Bible Conferences. It leads rather to the antiseptically secular protocols that govern what can be said—and especially what cannot be said—each evening on CBS News.

Comments

RICHARD D. LAND: I don't think Grant Wacker takes sufficient account of the disruptive influences of the Civil War. The Civil War removed from any meaningful participation in the political and cultural process of the country what had been, for over a century, the most intensely evangelical part of the United States. The South was a defeated enemy; and the nation's cultural, educational, social, and religious agenda was set by the victors, not by the vanquished. Lyndon Johnson was the first president elected after the Civil War who didn't have an accent, and he became president by virtue of an assassination. . . .

As a Southern Baptist, I think I know why many of you find Southern Baptists problematic. You have to understand us sociologically, rather than theologically. And in this country, Southern Baptists have behaved more like Catholics than like Protestants. We've been big enough to construct our own sort of alternative society, our own youth groups, our own schools. So we became, in our region, a kind of established religion in the same way that Catholicism was the "established" religion and social stabilizer for many immigrant groups. One result of this is that you have a lot of people who grow up Catholic or Southern Baptist, yet may not adhere to what Catholics and Southern Baptists have traditionally believed: they're cultural and historical Catholics, or cultural and historical Baptists.

JAMES DAVISON HUNTER: What all fundamentalists have in common is the populist suspicion that history has gone awry. And what has gone awry with history is modernity. "Modernity" means many things, obviously, but what fundamentalists share is the desire to make history "right" again. Continuity of institutions and leadership is not so important; what is essential is this central continuity of conviction—that something has gone wrong and that it has to be made right again. In other words, fundamentalism is

24

ultimately about history as narrative. Fundamentalism's power is its ability to define the story of faith in a national context. . . .

When I think about this, I'm reminded of Seymour Martin Lipset's *The Politics of Unreason*, which deals with so-called "radicalism" throughout history. One of the book's points is that the Christian Right, over the last century and a half and in its various forms, has succeeded in its response to modernity through failure. It has succeeded by having its own agenda institutionalized by parties (primarily political) that are larger than itself. The early stage of the Christian Right succeeded by its failure—its agenda was institutionalized by the Republican party in the 1980s. This institutionalization accounts, in part, for the disappearance of much of the first generation of the New Christian Right. But I think a new generation is taking shape and formulating a new agenda.

ROBERT BOOTH FOWLER: I think we also have to look at what we might call the "resources of power." And here I am struck by the contrast between the situation today and the Prohibition movement. The New Christian Right today is in a far weaker position than its predecessors, especially in terms of the elite culture and the media. Where evangelicals were "located" in class terms in the nineteenth century differed dramatically from where they are located today, which suggests to me that evangelicals had far greater chances of success then than now. In trying to understand the future of the New Christian Right, we cannot just compare its ideas with ideas from the past. We have to ask questions about class and about influence in the culture.

PAUL WEYRICH: Most people who comment on the evangelical movement picture it as an offensive movement politically. It is not. It is a *defensive* movement. The people who are involved in it didn't want to get involved; they got involved very reluctantly. They had accepted the notion (which may have taken root historically at the Scopes trial) that a good Christian would raise his family in the proper manner and would not participate very much in public life. If you did that, you could avoid all the corruption that was manifest in politics.

What changed all that was not the school-prayer issue, and it was not the abortion issue. I had discussions with all the leading lights of the movement in the late 1970s and early 1980s, post–*Roe* v. *Wade*, and they were all arguing that that decision was one more reason why Christians had to isolate themselves from the rest of the world. Certainly no Christian was going to have an abortion, and they could teach that to their children.

What caused the movement to surface was the federal government's moves against Christian schools. This absolutely shattered the Christian community's notion that Christians could isolate themselves inside their own institutions and teach what they pleased. The realization that they could not then linked up with the long-held conservative view that government is too powerful and intrusive, and this linkage was what made evangelicals active. It wasn't the abortion issue; that wasn't sufficient. It was the recognition that isolation simply would no longer work in this society.

When you look ahead, you should understand that the future of the larger culture will determine the future of the New Religious Right. This is not a cyclical movement in the way other political movements are. As long as cultural deterioration continues to manifest itself in horrible ways, evangelicals will be compelled to get active, even in ways that appall them. They'll feel absolutely obliged to do so. The realization that there are no enclaves in this society, that the government is going to come in and dictate how even churches behave, was what triggered the first enormous burst of energy and activity—and it will continue to spark it. After that, of course, the agenda of the Religious Right inevitably grows.

Richard D. Land is director of the Christian Life Commission of the Southern Baptist Convention; **James Davison Hunter** is professor of sociology and religious studies at the University of Virginia; **Robert Booth Fowler** is professor of political science at the University of Wisconsin in Madison; and **Paul Weyrich** is president of the Free Congress Foundation.

2

The Future of the Religious Right

Robert Wuthnow

HAVING observed with interest the so-called New Christian Right from its inception, I would like to speculate—from my vantage point as a sociologist—about the role it may play in American society in the 1990s and beyond. In doing so, I am mindful of the fact that most observers of American religion (and politics) were caught by surprise when the Religious Right emerged into national prominence in the late 1970s.[1] To make predictions now may be to shoot arrows off into the night with no better likelihood of hitting the mark than before. And yet we do know considerably more about the character and social location of the Religious Right now than we did when it first appeared. Perhaps this knowledge can be helpful in suggesting the directions it may take in the years ahead.

My approach will be to look back over the conditions that helped bring the New Christian Right into being, and to ask whether these conditions are likely to perpetuate it into the future or

Robert Wuthnow is Gerhard R. Andlinger Professor of Social Sciences and director of the Center for the Study of American Religion at Princeton University. His nine books include *The Struggle for America's Soul: Evangelicals, Liberals, and Secularism* and *Rediscovering the Sacred: Perspectives on Religion in Contemporary Society*.

whether they may be changing in ways that will alter its course. I do not assume that the Religious Right, or any social movement, is simply a product of the social conditions under which it emerges.[2] Indeed, many of these conditions are the accretions of the movement's own activities—its history, reputation, and repertoire of resources. The Religious Right, then, is not free to do entirely as it pleases. It cannot accomplish its goals by sheer dint of imagination. Rather, it has to adapt to its environment, garner resources, and respond to and challenge the issues with which it is confronted. These features of its interaction with the social environment we must try to understand.

We must pay heed to these conditions whether we are active leaders and supporters of the Religious Right, fellow travelers who feel that its aims somehow make a difference to our well-being, or opponents seeking ways to block its ambitions and aspirations. For my own part, I have been deeply concerned about the divisiveness in American religion to which the Religious Right has contributed. At the same time, some (perhaps much) of this divisiveness can be attributed to spokespersons in the wider society who understand little of the outlook and origins of the Religious Right. Examining the conditions that will guide the future trajectory of the Religious Right, therefore, is not so much a way of promoting its cause or aiding its enemies as of increasing our understanding of the society in which we live and the vital place of religious faith within this society.

In earlier works I have suggested a number of social conditions and processes that gave rise to the Religious Right or that produced some of the other characteristics of American religion and culture to which it responded.[3] As one attempts to account for something new that is still in the ascendancy, one is tempted to pay attention only to those factors that contribute positively to its rise. Other factors that may inhibit its further development, or even lead to its downfall, tend to be neglected. We are now at a critical juncture when a more balanced assessment of all these various factors needs to be made. In what follows I shall pay special attention to the social, cultural, and religious conditions that have proven particularly important in accounting for the rise of the Religious Right, but I shall also consider the nuances in these and other factors that may channel the Religious Right in various directions and augment or diminish its strength.

Before turning to this analysis, I wish to assert my disagreement with many casual observers of American culture who believe that the Religious Right is simply defunct. To be sure, the dissolution of the Moral Majority in 1989 and the eclipse of religious television, together with other developments in domestic and foreign politics in the 1990s, signal a moment of uncertainty in the fortunes of this movement. But most of the issues to which the movement has devoted attention remain unresolved, and there is still a strong core of leadership on which the movement can draw, as well as a loyal constituency.

Predisposing Circumstances

Analysts of social movements know the importance of looking at conditions that may, by themselves, have little to do with shaping a specific movement but in combination with other factors become enormously consequential. I believe there are at least three such characteristics of American religion generally that must be a part of any discussion of the Religious Right: the "this-worldly" orientation of American religion, its conviction that values matter, and its massive institutional resources.

The so-called "this-worldly" orientation of American religion (indeed, of Christianity in the modern West according to Max Weber) refers to its belief in the sanctity and significance of the present life, as opposed to the view in some religious traditions that only the life to come is important.[4] In American Christianity this orientation takes a variety of forms, from extreme beliefs holding that the life to come is simply a metaphor compared with the final reality of the present one, to various arguments about works in the present life leading to rewards in the afterlife, to concepts of God's kingdom and will for the earth. These variants are sometimes critical in channeling religious energies in specific directions. But the fact that American religion on the whole has an active orientation toward the present world is of the foremost significance. Historically, it has called believers to be concerned with the relation between faith and society. It encourages the faithful, individually and through their churches, to be interested in public affairs.

The Religious Right is an expression of this orientation in American Christianity. The movement itself is an effort to address social concerns from the standpoint of biblical teachings. It encourages its constituents to eschew a passive existence spent preparing for the life to come and to engage instead in active social service and moral reform. Thus engaged, the movement also becomes subject to the wider influences of the society in which it exists. The Religious Right does not try to isolate itself from the wider society; it confronts, engages, and resists. But in these very activities it exposes its flanks to broader political and cultural forces. Its this-worldly orientation, therefore, makes it more susceptible to many of the other social conditions that we shall consider presently.

It is, of course, peculiar to say that the Religious Right includes a this-worldly orientation, for many of its constituents are fundamentalists. And, of all religious groups in the United States, fundamentalists are generally thought to be the most other-worldly. Indeed, one of the hallmarks of American fundamentalism in the twentieth century has been its pre-millennial eschatology, a belief that envisions Christ's kingdom replacing the present age rather than coming into being through some evolution of the social order as we know it.[5] Why, if the present world is going to vanish in the twinkling of an eye, would fundamentalists care about political and moral reform?

The answer is varied, reflecting the diversity within American fundamentalism itself. Many leaders of the Religious Right, though fundamentalist in such beliefs as biblical inerrancy, have shifted toward a post-millennialist rather than a pre-millennialist eschatology. This view is especially pronounced in denominations with roots in Calvinism or the English Reformation, including Presbyterians and Baptists. It is also more characteristic of the more mainstream evangelicalism that appeared in the 1940s and 1950s than of sectarian fundamentalism. In other instances, pre-millennialism is still the eschatology of choice, but its other-worldliness has been tempered by doctrinal and practical considerations. Doctrinally, the pre-millennialism taught particularly in Baptist contexts holds that believers should prepare for the Second Coming of

Christ but avoid making specific predictions as to its date. In some teachings, believers are also encouraged to wage battle with the moral evils that may precipitate Armageddon and the end of the age, if only to allow more time for the heathen to be converted before the return of Christ. In other interpretations, dispensationalist theology has emphasized the age of the Church, during which God's work is to be conducted through the activities of believers in the Church. Practical and often cynical considerations having to do with pastoral ambitions, building programs, and fund-raising drives also enter the picture. Stated most crudely, large structures can only be justified by deferring the expected return of Jesus.[6]

These variations have, it should be noted, produced divisions within the ranks of the Religious Right and its potential constituents. Fundamentalists with a strong orientation toward inner piety and spirituality as a way of preparing for the day of the Lord are probably least active in New Right causes. Those with a strong sense of corporate warfare between the Church and forces of evil— and its apocalyptic implications—have probably been more active in the Religious Right. And those with Pentecostal orientations have probably been a mixed group. For some, an emphasis on the purification of the Church, as signified by the biblical account of Pentecost, has encouraged active efforts to resist evil and purify the wider society as well. For others, Pentecostal beliefs have led more toward a conception of inward renewal and personal holiness.

In the future the Religious Right will be enhanced by the overall this-worldliness of American religion, but also conditioned by doctrinal variations within this general orientation. Beliefs of such subtlety as to be little understood in the wider population will affect coalitions emerging across a broad spectrum of the Religious Right.

The seriousness with which values are taken in American religion is also an important predisposing factor, but one that can be dispensed with more easily. We have always believed that what a person is, believes, thinks, and values has an enormous impact not only on that person's behavior as an individual but also on the well-being of our society collectively. This is part of the individualism built into our culture and very much a feature of American religion as well. What the churches do, their teaching and preaching, makes a difference to the body politic because values count. Thus, it makes sense to worry not only about such things as poverty programs and national defense but also about the political implications of ethics, personal morality, what people read or see on television, and the values they learn in schools.[7]

When the Religious Right came into being, many public officials had ceased to show much concern about values, focusing instead on "structural" problems that required "policy" solutions. Even today, many in the universities think government programs are the only way to accomplish anything of importance. But the Religious Right was just one part of a broader effort in public life to renew attention on values. After Watergate, and then again with the numerous public scandals in the late 1980s, it became evident that values do make a difference. Leaders on the left as well as on the right began calling for closer consideration of values and morality in public life.

This reorientation is, however, a mixed blessing as far as the Religious Right itself is concerned. On the one hand, it will ensure that a large segment of the population believes that values, morality, and teachings, as opposed to purely structural solutions, do matter. On the other hand, when everyone—right and left—is talking about values, the distinctive claims of the Religious Right tend to be muted. With a less distinct identity its potential strength may be diminished.

The other predisposing condition I mentioned earlier—the massive institutional resources of American religion—refers to the fact that churches constitute a tremendous potential force in American society.[8] Were the Religious Right to attempt the same activities in, say, Sweden, it would be up against insuperable odds.[9] Clergy, church buildings, habits of religious giving, and participation in religious activities are too sparse there to give any religious movement much support. In the United States, however, things are vastly different.

For the immediate future, these resources are likely to remain in abundance. People join churches and attend Sunday worship services in about the same proportions as they did a generation ago.[10] But over the long haul, some diminution of these commitments seems likely. Though still only a minority, the number who claim no religious beliefs has grown steadily over the past two decades. A large proportion of our society also believes it is possible to be spiritual without any participation in organized religion.

One cannot simply conclude, however, that these trends will reduce the overall strength of the Religious Right. In the past, rising numbers of people without faith have generated controversies about religious beliefs being taught in schools or observed in public places. These controversies will likely continue, and will elicit reactions from the Religious Right. Whether 85 per cent of the public believes in God rather than 90 per cent, in short, will make less difference than whether the remaining 10 or 15 per cent is perceived to be a legal and educational threat to the rest.

Organizational Factors

While the cultural climate of American religion has important implications for the Religious Right so, too, does the way in which American religion is organized. I want to highlight three such factors: the declining significance of denominationalism, the role of special-purpose groups, and networks among religious leaders.

Over the past half century, denominationalism has declined seriously as the primary mode of identification in American religion. Indications of this decline include increased interfaith and interdenominational switching, heightened tolerance across faiths and denominational boundaries, ecumenical cooperation, and a de-emphasis in many denominations on distinctive teachings and specific membership requirements. This decline, I have argued elsewhere, helped clear the decks for the division that has emerged more recently in American religion between conservatives and liberals.[11] Relatively speaking, that division has been a more important source of identity and of public controversy because of the diminishing importance of other, crosscutting cleavages.

For the Religious Right, declining denominationalism has made it easier for mobilization to occur across group boundaries. Conservative Presbyterians and conservative Baptists were better able to join forces without denominational distinctions keeping them apart. A weakening of boundaries between the major faiths also made it possible for conservative Protestants to garner support from conservative Catholics and Jews.[12] The same was true on the liberal side of the fence.

Denominationalism seems likely to continue its decline in the foreseeable future. But the other side of the coin must also be examined. Churchgoers may care little about denominationalism, but clergy and church administrators care about it a great deal. Career opportunities, pension payments, and the policies of judicatories and legislative bodies depend on it. In the past few years, denominationalism actually seems to have been staging a minor revival, perhaps for these reasons. Conservative bodies, most notably the Southern Baptist Convention, have been struggling mightily over the theological destiny of their denominations, and liberal bodies, such as the Episcopal, Presbyterian, and Methodist churches, have launched evangelism campaigns in an effort to regain membership losses.[13]

If this revival of denominationalism were to continue, it would, I believe, have two significant implications for the Religious Right. One would be a reduction in the energy available for its activities: in conservative denominations because more energy would be spent fighting internal battles; and in liberal denominations because more attention would be devoted to causes, such as evangelism and church growth, that conservatives could espouse. The other implication is that denominational organizations would continue to provide a staging ground, if a more decentralized one, for the political and moral campaigns of the Religious Right.

The second organizational factor bearing on the Religious Right is the development of special-purpose groups. Special-purpose groups are the religious counterpart of interest groups in American politics. Their number has grown considerably over the past quarter century and is likely to continue growing. Organized around the particular aims of a cohort of like-minded people, these groups do not try to unite a heterogeneous body of believers in the way churches do. Consequently, special-purpose groups potentially contribute to the separation of believers into those championing conservative causes and those espousing liberal causes. In the past conservative special-purpose groups have played an important role in the work of the Religious Right.[14]

Newspaper stories about special-purpose groups (a Christian

Bikers' Association for motorcycle enthusiasts, for example) suggest that special-purpose groups are continuing to flourish. But one of the distinctive characteristics of these groups is that they come and go as interests change. Compared with denominations and even local congregations, they are inherently unstable. The Religious Right, therefore, cannot count on these groups for indefinite support. Rather, energy will have to be expended to start new groups that reflect changing issues and interests as old groups pass out of existence.

The question has also arisen, given the polarization in American religion of conservative and liberal factions, whether special-purpose groups might just as well try to bridge the gap, rather than contribute to it. They can, of course, try. But my own interviews and informal conversations with leaders of special-purpose groups suggest a doubtful prognosis. In part, the problem is ideological. To pursue an objective zealously, one has to believe zealously in its truth. The leader of one group told me, when you know you're right, why should you compromise? And another person stated in a letter to me, "mixing gasoline and water" isn't going to get you where you need to go. But the problem is also strategic. Special-purpose groups depend on having a clear objective and a distinct constituency. When challenged to use less divisive language, the leader of a liberal group told me, "I see your point, but we know what language our contributors respond to." For these reasons, I doubt that the efforts of special-purpose groups, either on the right or the left, will be much diminished by new groups trying to take more moderate positions.

The third organizational factor we must understand is networks among religious leaders. The origin of the New Christian Right owed much to pre-existing networks of independent Baptist clergy who could be pressed into service as state and local chairmen of the Moral Majority. Denominationalism, in this case, contributed positively, rather than negatively, to the movement's initial success.[15]

These networks, I suspect, will be increasingly important in the future. National campaigns have proven enormously expensive in the past, and these costs will be harder to cover if religious television ceases to be an effective revenue-generating mechanism. Moreover, such campaigns have tended to produce adverse publicity in the national press and have resulted in relatively few legislative or judicial victories in Washington. Indeed, the thrust of many legislative bills and court cases has been to press action back onto the state and local levels. And this is precisely where clergy networks can be valuable. Presbyteries, synods, and regional associations bring clergy into contact with one another. Through these contacts they can coordinate efforts without a massive centralized organization in the nation's capital.

Sources of Societal Strain

Thus far, I have concentrated largely on factors and conditions that may be thought of as potential resources for the Religious Right. But resources make very little difference unless there is some crisis or grievance against which to deploy them. We need to say more about how broad characteristics of American religion translate into actual movement resources. But first, we must consider some of the changes in our society that have resulted in crises—or at least strains—capable of generating responses from the religious community. For brevity's sake, I will concentrate on the effects of educational expansion, the welfare state, and upheavals in domestic politics.

Educational expansion was, as we know, extraordinarily rapid in the 1960s and 1970s. Increasing numbers of students went off to college and, perhaps as much from "going off" as from actually going to college, adopted a more liberal, secular, and privatized religious orientation. As recently as the mid-1980s, college attendance was the most significant social predictor of religious liberalism.[16] Thus, some of the fervor of the Religious Right registered a class dimension as well: the educationally disadvantaged struck out against the pretensions of the educationally advantaged, to put it in the crudest terms.

But educational expansion has slowed remarkably since the 1970s. Going away to college, moreover, now puts young people in a less turbulent environment than it did in the 1960s and 1970s. Campus cultures have become more conservative or at least more business oriented, and there is less rethinking of basic familial values as a result. Furthermore, the move into higher education among religious conservatives has had important consequences of its own. At present, religious conservatives can scarcely be distinguished from religious liberals as far as levels of educational attainment are concerned.[17]

What does all this imply for the Religious Right? As with some of the other developments I have mentioned, the probable consequences are mixed. Over the long haul, higher education does seem to have a liberalizing and relativizing effect, which may shift many of the Right's potential constituents toward a moderate, middle-of-the-road, live-and-let-live orientation. In the short term, though, the rising educational levels of religious conservatives constitute a net plus for the Religious Right. Better-educated people are more likely to vote, have more money to give to causes of their choice, tend to be more active in community and political organizations, read and keep abreast of societal issues, and provide leadership skills. Moreover, their educational parity with religious liberals is apt to engender some discontent over their social position. Religious conservatives are still more likely to have come from educationally disadvantaged backgrounds, to live in regions of the country where educational opportunities are less available, to have attended less prestigious institutions, and to have majored in more technical and practical subjects. For all these reasons they are bound to feel at least some resentment toward those who have been more privileged.[18] Resentment, of course, is not the only factor in Religious Right mobilization. But it surely has been one and will likely continue to be.

The welfare state grew rapidly during the 1960s and 1970s just as higher education did. In taxation, regulation, court cases, defense, welfare provision, health, education, and the formulation of public policy more generally, government became a more intrusive element in everyday life.[19] Consequently, groups wanting to achieve a goal increasingly organized themselves to press government with their demands. Groups opposing prevailing tendencies did too. The Religious Right was generally suspicious of big government and its various social programs. But to oppose this political entity, the Religious Right had to organize as a political entity itself.

On the surface, the right (religious and secular) during the 1980s can be seen as having successfully curtailed the bureaucratic welfare state. Ronald Reagan came to office on an anti-government ticket. Regulatory agencies were dismantled; taxes were reformed; free enterprise was extolled. For all this, however, the period witnessed very little actual government reduction. New programs replaced older ones; the same was true of taxes. Big government, it seems, has become a way of life. And it will continue to be in the future.

The Religious Right will probably continue to play a game of insider-outsider with government (a topic that merits consideration on its own). And it will probably be more effective in mobilizing support by posing as an outsider rather than an insider. American religion, after all, has a broad tradition of skepticism toward big government. But something akin to the Religious Right—that is, a religio-*political* organization—will probably also continue into the indefinite future. A politicized, government-dominated society will, in short, produce a politicized religion.

Unlike higher education or the bureaucratic state, upheaval in domestic politics is not a phenomenon showing linear growth. It refers instead to the instability or cyclical dynamic in American politics. Religious Right leaders were influential in the past because some of their issues and some of their champions rose to prominence. At the same time this dynamism in American politics introduces much uncertainty into the fortunes of such a movement. One has only to mention the different religio-political styles of Jimmy Carter and Ronald Reagan, or Newt Gingrich and Dan Quayle, to see the significance of this uncertainty. Unexpected military crises, Supreme Court decisions, and deaths add to the unpredictability of American politics.

My point here is that the Religious Right came into being partly in response to upheavals produced by the civil-rights movement, the Vietnam War, and the 1973 Supreme Court decision on abortion. Similar upheavals in the future could greatly augment, or greatly diminish, the strength of the Religious Right.

Resources That Can Be Mobilized

Having considered some aspects of the broad social environment, we can now turn more specifically to the Religious Right as a movement. Its effectiveness has depended on its ability to muster the resources necessary to respond to its environment, and to respond in such a way that sometimes transforms this environment. Rather than viewing the Religious Right as a monolithic entity, therefore, we need to focus on its specific resources, asking how each component of its overall apparatus may fare in the years ahead.

At the risk of neglecting some important components, let us focus on several that may be particularly subject to the vagaries of social change: people with sympathetic orientations, grass-roots leaders, a nationally visible elite, communications media, time and money, and the wielders of power.

A broad base of people with sympathetic orientations is important to any movement, even if only a small minority ever becomes active in the movement. The Religious Right has depended heavily on such a base for financial contributions, letters and petitions, votes, and symbolic support such as that registered in opinion polls. Although relatively small numbers ever expressed outright support for the Moral Majority, for example, a much larger proportion of the public paid lip-service to the issues it embraced, such as pro-life policies, the campaign against pornography and sexual permissiveness, and a strong national defense.[20] At present, this base of support seems fairly secure. Polls suggest that there are at least as many people, if not more, identifying themselves as religious conservatives now as there were in the past.[21] Studies also indicate a strong interest in pro-family issues, concern about sexual infidelity, and a commitment to traditional standards of honesty and integrity.

Grass-roots leaders are plentiful as well. Despite a general decline in voter participation and involvement in partisan activities, the American public continues to be actively engaged in a wide variety of volunteer efforts. Clergy can play an especially prominent role as grass-roots leaders. So can laity with special skills, such as lawyers and business elites. The public often misjudged the Religious Right in the past, thinking of it as a gathering of misguided hillbillies without the savvy to accomplish anything.[22] With rising levels of education and an additional decade of political experience, its ability to organize itself effectively at the grass-roots level will be even greater.

A nationally visible elite was created for the Religious Right around such figures as Jerry Falwell and Pat Robertson. With Falwell's retreat from politics and Robertson's anemic showing in the 1988 presidential campaign, serious questions need to be asked about the future of this elite. Certainly, individual names can be put forward as possible successors to the national leadership. But these individuals may also experience relatively short-lived public careers. The question, therefore, is not who they will be but from which category of persons they will be selected.

Let me venture two guesses. First, the history of the Religious Right itself and what we know from public opinion more broadly suggest that the future figurehead of the Religious Right probably should not come from the parish clergy. Falwell was always limited by the demands of his own church and by the view that he was sectarian because of his Baptist identity. Television ministers like Robertson and Billy Graham have been able to reach wider audiences because they are manifestly less sectarian. But even Robertson had difficulty bridging the gap between pulpit and politics. One can think of writers, counselors, lobbyists, and business people who might have greater success.[23] Second, it proved in both these cases a handicap that the national leadership was speaking so clearly in the accents of the American South. Though the strongest constituency of the Religious Right is located in the southern Bible Belt, its audience is sufficiently diverse that a leader from Washington, D.C., or California, or the great Midwest would probably be a better choice.

Communications media have been tremendously important for the Religious Right. Direct-mail solicitations using computerized mailing lists helped it come into being in the first place. Magazines, newsletters, and radio played a role too. But it was clearly religious television that gave the movement its widest exposure.[24] People with doctrinal sympathies watched and—unfazed by the hand-waving, shouting, angry rhetoric, and emotional display—found support for their social, moral, and political concerns. But others watched as well. And they came away with a deeply negative impression. The very style was wrong for them. For people conditioned to watching "Johnny Carson" and "Family Ties," such broadcasts of religious fervor seemed embarrassingly strange. This, together with the fact that secular-television commentators and news people became the natural interpreters of religious television, made it a remarkably divisive force in American religion.[25]

Had the Religious Right not enjoyed the technologies of religious television, it might never have become the powerful movement it did. But eventually the time came to pay the piper. Like a bubble on Wall Street that turned people into instant millionaires, and just as quickly bankrupted them, religious television made and nearly unmade the Religious Right in a few short years. Not only did it strike an axe through the center of American religion, but it also made the Religious Right itself far too vulnerable to the vices of a Jimmy Swaggart or a Jim and Tammy Faye Bakker, and concentrated too much power in the hands of Jerry Falwell and Pat Robertson.

In the future, therefore, we might ask whether the Religious Right would be better served by opting for quieter media. Traditionally, the churches have made a serious impact on American culture by preaching and teaching, by training children in basic religious values, by sustaining people in the religious community itself, and by augmenting these activities with books, magazines, tracts, and personal visitation. Doing things this way may seem slow and old-fashioned in an age of television. But while television evokes quick responses, it transmits little in the way of enduring commitments. Perhaps Jerry Falwell, in turning his attention to teaching and preaching, came again to that realization.

Time and money are the most tangible resources the Religious Right must mobilize to be effective. As I have already suggested, these may be more plentiful in the future as religious conservatives move up the social ladder educationally and professionally. Benefits may even derive from the movement of the baby-boomer generation into retirement, although this will obviously depend on how large a proportion of this generation holds conservative religious views. The women's movement will perhaps be the major limiting factor for the Religious Right, which in the past has relied heavily on women for voluntary labor both for the churches and for political activities organized by the churches. In the future more women will have economic responsibilities in the labor force, and thus fewer will be available for these voluntary activities. It is little wonder that the Religious Right has often adopted issues that discourage women's inclusion in the labor force.

The wielders of power, finally, are a very decisive factor in the fate of a movement such as the Religious Right. We cannot over emphasize the significance of Ronald Reagan's personal role in embracing religious broadcasters, giving moral support to the conservative clergy, and drawing Religious Right leaders into his administration. Reagan was sincere in these efforts, even if not a great deal of substance was accomplished as a result. We hear a lot from political analysts about the variations in presidential styles. Perhaps a religious movement headed by television preachers was the perfect match for a president known as the "great communicator." But we may well imagine that the different styles of other presidents might require a different sort of movement.

Factors That Dampen Movements

I have touched earlier on factors, such as a shrinking constituency, that may dampen the fortunes of the Religious Right in the future. Declining institutional resources in American religion, a preoccupation with denominational squabbles, and the relativism that results when more people attend college may sodden the hopes of movement leaders in some general way. But there are also some things that movements do themselves—which in retrospect may be seen as having driven nails into their own coffins.

One that we might not think of immediately is the problem of winning. Suppose the Religious Right achieved all its goals. It would then have no reason to exist. This prospect seems remote. But suppose abortions were completely outlawed and prayer and Bible-reading were returned to the schools as mandated policy. What then?

I raise this prospect partly to suggest that the Religious Right may well diminish in the future because it has already achieved some of its purposes. Jerry Falwell could perhaps disband the Moral Majority in good faith by asserting that it had succeeded in placing moral issues on the public agenda in a serious way. But I also want to insert a more cynical note. Most movements, I believe, never really hope to accomplish their stated objectives. Nobody was more surprised than Lenin when the Bolsheviks were swept into power in 1917. And nobody would be more surprised than Jerry Falwell if the Supreme Court suddenly reversed itself on all the issues the Moral Majority had opposed. The Religious Right, like other movements, has pursued some objectives in the hope of achieving others. The Family Protection Act might never pass, but championing it will at least have brought family issues to the public's attention. In the future the Religious Right will have to adopt similar strategies if it hopes to perpetuate itself. Always champion specific policies that remain just beyond reach. Returning prayer to the schoolroom might well be a good issue to pursue.

The only thing that may be worse for a social movement than winning is losing. (Although sometimes losing may not even be as bad as winning: for example, Prohibition was probably worse for the temperance movement than its repeal.) But suppose a movement does lose. What if case after case goes through the courts, each one telling the Religious Right that it was on the wrong side after all? We love winning enough that such a string of defeats would undoubtedly ferret out a lot of the movement's fair-weather friends. It would not, however, signal the end of the movement.

Were the Religious Right somehow to lose, either through actual defeat or because other issues were taking priority on the public stage, I suspect it would not so much die as retreat into quieter pastures. A different scenario is certainly possible. When the student counterculture began to die in the early 1970s, its dissolution was accompanied by the birth of a variety of off-beat, more radical, even violent offshoots, such as Synanon and the Symbionese Liberation Army. We might see the Religious Right dissolving into radical clusters of skin-heads, neo-Nazis, and self-appointed destroyers of adult bookstores and NC-17-rated movies. But I doubt it. That specter has been put forth by the press. But it betrays only misunderstanding of the religious roots of the movement. Its constituents are largely law-abiding, white, middle-class suburbanites whose jobs, not to mention their religious upbringing, deter them from going more than ten miles over the speed limit, let alone committing a felony.[26]

The more likely outcome is that old Religious Righters will retreat to quieter pastures, namely the Church itself. Long after the repeal of Prohibition, temperance advocates quietly sent in petitions from their churches. The rallies and saloon-smashing ended; the petitions did not. In this sense, the Religious Right may have a long future indeed.

Short of such unlikely events as total success or defeat, the Religious Right may also find itself weakened in the future by crosscutting issues. During the 1980s the Religious Right became a powerful force in American religion partly because the issues it embraced—pro-life, anti-pornography, anti-homosexuality, opposition to the Equal Rights Amendment, and a few others—all neatly overlapped. People who supported one plank of the right's platform generally supported others as well. The same had not been true in the 1960s. Then, religious people were active on both sides of the civil-rights movement and on both sides of the anti-war movement. But the two issues cut in somewhat different ways religiously. People who agreed on one often disagreed on the other.[27]

The intrusion of some new issue on the public agenda could weaken the Religious Right in the same way. Without the strong regional differences between North and South that were brought to the surface by the civil-rights movement in the 1960s, however, this is less likely. Most issues at present would fall along the lines already in place. Nevertheless, the Religious Right must be careful, for these lines are always somewhat fluid, as the secular right has found to its dismay.

Finally, the Religious Right always runs the danger of being weakened by internal disputes. Some observers of the Pat Robertson candidacy in 1988 believed his chances were limited by the fact that Falwell supporters tended not to turn themselves energetically in Robertson's direction.[28] Other divisions will continue to haunt the Religious Right. Creedal fundamentalists who place heavy emphasis on the rational aspects of the Bible are often skeptical of Pentecostals who pride themselves on emotion. White fundamentalists have largely failed to enlist black fundamentalists in their cause. Protestants and Catholics, for all their affinities on issues of abortion and pornography, are still divided on other grounds. This is not to say that the constituency of the Religious Right may not, indeed, be a "moral majority." But neither is it the monolithic specter that liberal critics have often made it out to be.

A Cautious Forecast

In conclusion, then, let me state again the uncertainty with which any forecasts are made, and offer what seems to be a plausible scenario for the Religious Right in the years ahead. In this scenario a strong sector of the American population will remain firmly committed to the churches and will want a society in which moral values are respected. This constituency will be composed primarily of white middle-class suburbanites, many of whom are in the lower echelons of the middle class but an increasing number of whom will be college-educated professionals. Most will have families and be devoted to the virtues of the nuclear family. Some will be mobilized by fear—fear that religion is being pushed from the political arena, fear that the pious are in danger of disenfranchisement, fear that the truly moral are being marginalized by the forces of anarchy and social decay. But the majority will participate in politics from a sense of entitlement, knowing that religion has a rightful place in American politics as long as it is willing to play by the rules of democracy—"a right to a stall," as Hodding Carter has written, "to many stalls, in the civic marketplace."[29]

The leadership will be centered in the local churches but connected locally and regionally through clergy networks and alliances among special-purpose groups. At the local level the Religious Right will work to keep their schools strong, their communities clean, and their politicians from swaying too far to the left.

Though this scenario sounds in many ways like the Religious Right of the present, it differs in the character of its organization at the national level. It will perhaps be headed by a Christian author or administrator without denominational or regional limitations. It will, above all, be more decentralized and less visible to the public at large.[30] Some of its branches will work at lobbying in the nation's capital. Others will seek to influence state legislatures and municipal councils. Still others will fight legal battles, though few of these cases will reach the Supreme Court and fewer still will be decided on grounds that set far-reaching national precedents. In other words, the courts themselves will encourage a more decentralized style of political action in the future. In addition—although this is perhaps only wishful thinking—the Religious Right of the future will be less concerned with achieving its ends through politics alone and more devoted to the ideals of service, caring for the poor and disadvantaged, promoting community, reconciliation, and the transmission of values through teaching and training the young.

Response

James Davison Hunter

IF there is an abiding myth among members of the New Religious Right, it concerns the paramount importance of values. In their view, the problems we face at the end of the twentieth century are a consequence of people's having bad values, that is, of their making wrong choices. The solution to our problems at the end of the twentieth century, therefore, is finding people with good values, and getting them to assert themselves in public life.

This is somewhat akin to a father telling his daughter, "You can be whatever you set your mind on being when you grow up." Like him, we hope it is true, but the chance of anyone's son or daughter becoming president, or a senator, or a CEO depends on certain conditions—material conditions such as class, race, region of origin, and the structure of opportunities. These factors influence even the girl's imagination of what she could aspire to be. While it is true that values do have consequences, they are not the only things that have consequences. There are other factors over which human agency has little or no control. I think this is the significance of Wuthnow's essay.

If one expanded the father-and-daughter metaphor, one might assign Wuthnow the role of the family friend who calmly interjects a measure of reality into the girl's hopes and dreams: "Yes dear, you know how much I love you and support you, too, but let us face the facts—your father is a bricklayer; you have been to poor schools; and the kids you hang around with are heading nowhere. The likelihood that you will be president or a Supreme Court justice, then, is minimized by certain material conditions of your existence."

James Davison Hunter is professor of sociology and religious studies at the University of Virginia and author of *Culture Wars: The Struggle to Define America* and *Evangelicalism: The Coming Generation*.

Wuthnow outlines the material and cultural conditions that provide the parameters within which the discussion of the Religious Right future really needs to take place. He does this very well and convincingly. He brings to this discussion a knowledge of the conditions that have informed and made possible such ideological revolutions as the Reformation, the Enlightenment, and nineteenth-century socialism.

I wish to comment briefly on the conditions that Wuthnow has already set forth. To do this, I would like to step back, recast the terms of discussion, and go directly to the concept of the "New Religious Right." Used in the 1980s by academics, policy-makers, and activists to describe the events, fissures, and controversies of that period, the concept of the New Religious Right is a political concept. What I would like to highlight is that it is a political concept describing a reality and a conflict that is, at root, *not* political. The concept, New Right, presupposes a continuum of right to left, wherein Jerry Falwell and Pat Robertson are on one side, the National Council of Churches and other activists are on the other, and millions of people are somewhere in the middle. What this notion presupposes is that people are actually operating on the same plane of moral and political discussion.

As a way of recasting the discussion, I would argue that there is something deeper at play. George Weigel has used the concept of *kulturkampf*, and the title of my own book is *Culture Wars: The Struggle to Define America*. I would argue that the division we have seen through the late 1970s, 1980s, and into the 1990s is not just political but cultural—part of a culture war. It is a conflict that deals with fundamental assumptions, ideals, and obligations; fundamental moral commitments; our conception of good and evil; and our understanding of what is, and what is not, to be tolerated in our communities. The image of a continuum, then, is not really an accurate image in my opinion. The language of politics is not the most accurate way of describing the conflict in which the New Christian Right (NCR) has been involved. Rather than a continuum, I think we are talking about spheres or even solar systems—which is why the main actors are talking past one another in so many issues of public discourse. They are not talking on the same plane of moral and political discourse. They are operating within fundamentally different cosmologies and worldviews.

While Wuthnow downplays the nature of alliances between conservative Catholics, evangelical Protestants, and orthodox Jews probably for institutional reasons, I believe these alliances should be played up for symbolic reasons, to show that the battles are ultimately about different conceptions of the "good" society, about the meaning of America, and even more about the future of Western civilization. What ultimately divides the NCR and the larger orthodox alliance from its opponents are fundamentally different conceptions of moral authority. Mormons, Moonies, fundamentalists, conservative Catholics, and orthodox Jews all share in common a belief that moral authority derives from transcendent sources. Actors on the progressivist side hold the belief that moral authority derives from inner-worldly sources, from what I call self-grounded rational discourse. At one level, what is really going on here is a referendum on the meaning of the Enlightenment.

In this light, I would argue that the conflict of the late 1970s, 1980s, and early 1990s is really the second major stage of this larger conflict. The first stage was aptly symbolized by the Scopes trial of 1925. That trial was largely a referendum on theological and moral authority. In essence, the question faced there was how do we decide what is ultimately true? Though the fundamentalists legally won in Dayton, Tennessee, the net effect was a colossal loss for the forces of orthodoxy. When the conflict over theology had been settled, the orthodox alliance, primarily the evangelical-fundamentalist contingent, came to terms with its theological cognitive minority status throughout the 1930s, 1940s, and 1950s. Many of the assumptions of the nineteenth-century Victorian and Protestant worldview were still, however, largely taken for granted. The challenge of the 1960s, therefore, which ignited the battles of the 1970s and 1980s, and continues to fuel controversy in the 1990s, is really a second phase, or second component, of this larger conflict over the values of bourgeois civilization. This, I believe, is the last battle.

How does a recasting of the terms of discussion bear on the debate about the future of the Religious Right? One of the problems of the NCR and the larger orthodox alliance through the

1980s has been that its leadership has defined the problem and the solution as *political* in nature. Such views are articulated in common refrains: "If we could only get enough Christian politicians into office . . . if we could only overturn *Roe* v. *Wade* . . . if we could only get Robert Bork onto the Supreme Court . . . or if we could only pressure networks to get 'anti-family' programming off the air, then *all* would be well." But if the conflict in which the NCR is engaged is *cultural*, then the NCR has not addressed the real problems but rather its symptoms—symbols of the real problem.

I would argue that the NCR has been more concerned with enforcing public morality through legal and political means than with cultivating public virtue. But if the conflict is cultural rather than political, the question is: what are the *cultural* resources, conditions, and settings that the orthodox alliance needs to deal with? How well is it mobilizing these larger cultural resources for cultural ends, with the object of redefining the fundamental assumptions that prevail in our society (changing, for example, the way people think about unborn human life)?

At this level we see the significance of competing knowledge industries. The knowledge production of the orthodox alliance is very impressive. The book-publishing industry of the evangelical world is a multi-million-dollar industry. The expansion of home schooling and private Christian schooling is part of this larger knowledge industry. But knowledge production of the secular cultural establishment, what some call the "new class," almost completely eclipses that of the Religious Right. Moreover, the orthodox alliance's knowledge industry, for all its appeal to middle America, is largely ghettoized. Evangelical and Catholic authors stick to their own publishing houses and preach to their own choirs, and do not address the prevailing secular orthodoxies promulgated by the secular knowledge class.

What does this mean for the future? As long as the leadership of the orthodox alliance defines the problems of the late twentieth century as political, we are going to see a series of successes and failures. The culture war is not a monolithic battle; it is a wide range of discrete skirmishes (e.g., domestic partners in San Francisco, textbooks in Tennessee), and I do not believe that either side will win or lose. I believe there will be a series of wins and losses across the board. Wuthnow suggests that we are moving into the second generation of this phenomenon. The first generation of leadership has largely disappeared, and we are seeing a new one, utilizing a decentralized form of political action. The *Webster* decision of the Supreme Court becomes a symbol of the general political strategies of the Religious Right. Because their strategies remain political (even if they are decentralized), they will have a marginal impact in bringing about the changes in American society they really desire.

Comments

EDWARD G. DOBSON: The Religious New Right did not start because of a concern about abortion. I want to go back and re-emphasize that. I sat in the non-smoke-filled back room with the Moral Majority, and I frankly do not remember abortion ever being mentioned as a reason why we ought to do something.

I think there was a perceived threat, but not the singular threat, of what the government was going to do to Christian schools that prompted the activism. I think a series of threats, broadly described as "secular humanism," caused a community that had been separatist for fifty years to act. It acted because, all of a sudden, the larger secular world was having an impact on their members' "separated" lives, through gays-rights issues, moral erosion in the public schools, banning prayer in the schools, and government interference in Christian schools. That complex of issues brought the evangelical coalition back together again, publicly and actively, in a defensive reaction. This coalition attempted to preserve the integrity of our organizations. . . .

Has the Religious New Right been successful? Yes and no. It has shaped the debate on moral issues; it has promoted Christian citizenship; it has formed many subgroups that continue to exert influence in the culture. As a pastor, however, I think it was a failure because people in the community of faith do not seem to hold values much different from those of the wider culture.

The future of the New Religious Right may well be connected to the 40-and-under generation. In the church I serve, 69 per cent of the adults who attend are 40 years old or younger. And when I look at them, I realize that they're not all that concerned with obscenity or all that exercised about abortion. Those are not issues for the average person 40 years old or younger. They may be significant, important issues, but with a few exceptions, I don't see them as significant, important issues for most people in the congregation I serve, who are more concerned with issues of materialism, poverty, justice, the environment, and personal commitment to

Christ. If the 40-and-younger people are the future of the Religious New Right, I don't see much of a future. . . .

The Religious New Right was a disenfranchised movement, a countercultural movement not accepted by any of the cultural elites or the mainstream. When President Reagan embraced the evangelicals, leaders like Jerry Falwell assumed that this legitimized a movement that had been demeaned, ignored, and branded as "double-knit, Appalachian, pew-jumping, holy-roller, anachronistic, white-socks," and all that. Once we got into the White House, we thought "we are now legitimate because we are now equal partners." But we never were. Many put on 100 per cent wool suits and became politicized by the activist process but, as a consequence, lost some of their impact.

PAUL WEYRICH: The Religious New Right had an enormous opportunity to change the situation in America, politically if not culturally, but it utterly failed to do so. And the reasons why aren't the reasons I always read about. The Religious New Right failed, first of all, because it had a ghetto mentality about what it was. Immediately after Ronald Reagan was elected (with the Republican leader in the Senate being Howard Baker and the White House chief of staff being Jim Baker), the administration announced that its social agenda would have to be postponed for several years. In response to that blow, evangelical and fundamentalist leaders refused to say anything. Imagine a President Cuomo getting elected with the help of the civil-rights movement and then announcing that civil-rights issues were nonsense and he wasn't even going to address them. We all know what the ensuing activity would be like.

Well, I had a conference call with the leadership of the Religious New Right at the time of the Reagan announcement, and I said: "This cannot be tolerated. If the idea that economic issues are more important than moral issues takes hold, then it says something about what we stand for." The leaders told me that I was much too harsh and that they rather agreed with the notion that economic issues were important. They thought Reagan had a good point, that he had to deal with the economy first. I'm not a theologian; I'm a politician. But I'm talking to people who are supposed to be theologians and telling them, "No, you settle matters that pertain to God first—that's the proper order." I was told, "No, absolutely not, we have to have credibility first," and so on.

What overshadowed all their concerns was simply their pleasure in being able to get in even the back door of the White House. They didn't want to do anything to jeopardize that. They were willing to put aside what minimalistic ideas they had on their so-called "agendas"—and with the exception of their pro-life position, they were trivial—to safeguard meaningless access.

It was at this point that I began to talk about the necessity for a profound shift. Yet I found a lack of comprehension on the part of a lot of people. . . . Today, I think the movement is maturing a little bit. I see a greater interest in a more comprehensive agenda. I'm seeing things taken more seriously by, for example, the Southern Baptists. I'm seeing a different quality of leadership, one that doesn't want to just jump in and get a headline but that wants to take a long, slow look at what can be done in the overall picture. And that's very encouraging. Some people have emerged who have the capability of understanding the necessity of a truly serious agenda, one aimed at the culture and not just at the political world. Changing the politics without changing the culture won't succeed.

KENNETH MYERS: The Religious New Right underestimates the way in which style and culture animate its adversaries. In a late-1970s *Village Voice* article about Jerry Falwell, there was a very interesting spin. The writer for the *Voice* was primarily offended by Falwell's suit. The double-knit factor was far more frightening than any political offense Falwell had committed. I think these people were afraid that Falwell was out to make the world safe for Lawrence Welk. . . .

Why doesn't anyone start a Christian Endowment for the Arts? What if some proportion of what is spent fighting Serrano and Mapplethorpe were spent on supporting painters, poets, and com-posers who we believe are sustaining the Western tradition? There are material realities, not just values, that propel and sustain a culture. This cannot be emphasized too much. Our values will make sense in the second, third, and fourth generation only if there are material structures in the culture that make those values sensible.

JAMES DAVISON HUNTER: If I were to advise the leadership of the "orthodox" alliance, I would say that, while it is appropriate to pursue a legal strategy giving priority to the modification of *Roe v. Wade*, it is not enough to change the law. Laws require legitimacy and, therefore, a grass-roots strategy is necessary as well—a changing of hearts and minds. Moreover, in between the legal strategy and the grass-roots strategy, there needs to be a cultural strategy. Cultural problems require cultural solutions, not just political solutions. And the goal of the cultural strategy should be to make abortion seem unthinkable.

Edward G. Dobson is senior pastor of Calvary Church, Grand Rapids, Michigan; **Paul Weyrich** is president of the Free Congress Foundation; **Kenneth Myers** is editor-in-chief of the *Stewardship Journal*; and **James Davison Hunter** is professor of sociology and religious studies at the University of Virginia.

3

The Failure of
the Religious Right

Robert Booth Fowler

I N discussing evangelicalism today and in the future, I will focus
on the movement called the New Christian Right (NCR), a
movement that was deeply intertwined with evangelical and fundamentalist elements in American religion. My argument is that it
failed, and failed badly, and that there are lessons for the future
about evangelicalism and politics that may be learned from this
experience. To learn these lessons, one must also explore *why* the
New Christian Right failed.

I do not claim that my interpretation is self-evident. Far from it.
I recognize that there are several other serious and plausible views,
and I propose to argue with them. It is time to take stock, and I
propose to try to do so.

The story of the Moral Majority, the late Moral Majority, and the
larger New Christian Right is not over, is perhaps far from over.
But it is not difficult to describe the movement as something of a
summer flower only. Although no exact date can be cited for its
origins, there is no doubt that by 1979–1980 it was under way.

Robert Booth Fowler is a professor of political science at the University
of Wisconsin in Madison and author of *Religion and Politics in America, A
New Engagement: Evangelical Political Thought, 1966–1976*, and *Unconven-
tional Partners: Religion and Liberal Culture in the United States.*

The history of the movement is interesting and will surely engage more than a few historians in the future.[1] The contrast between the mood in 1980 and that in 1990 may well be noted. That contrast suggests the failure.

Consider the difference between 1990 and the early 1980s, the time of mobilization and certainly the point of discovery by the national media. Mirror images played everywhere with the consistent message that something called the New Christian Right was on the march. *Time* and *Newsweek*, ever-dependable trumpets for the latest ideas and fashions of the elite culture, announced the rise of the Moral Majority and similar organizations.[2] *The New Yorker* proclaimed the word to its sophisticates about the "disciplined, charging army" of the New Right.[3] Hysteria heightened into a culture war as both sides pressed forward.[4]

But there were skeptics, particularly among social scientists, who went beyond the rhetoric to gather some data or to review history and who had the sense to sift through both. Resisting the initial waves of consternation over the New Christian Right in social-science circles, they raised doubts about how easy it would be to alter as established and stable a culture as ours. They questioned extravagant claims made about the NCR's impact on the electoral process and elsewhere. But I think that their doubts did not command attention easily or quickly.[5]

Defining Evangelicalism

Before going on, I need to try to define both the New Christian Right and evangelicalism, which is the source of most of the support for the New Christian Right. Rivers of ink have already been spent on what evangelicalism might mean and how the New Christian Right might be grasped.

The public-opinion road—with its surveys, agreements and disagreements, and problems of nuance and intensity—has accomplished much in terms of defining evangelicalism according to popular usage, refined by scholarly reflection. The resulting definition often accents inerrant Scripture, commitment to evangelism, and, of course, salvation through Jesus alone.[6] Within that rough context there is a tremendous amount of data on evangelicalism.[7]

A more cultural approach is less interested in doctrines than in networks of people, churches, publications, even summer camps. Such an approach is, in fact, a vital supplement to any examination of the evangelical world, which is a world, not a set of abstract beliefs. It is, moreover, a self-conscious world, one whose members know they belong to it, albeit with all the reservations and uncertainties we all have with similar cultural definitions of self. Using this perspective, we may say that evangelicalism is defined by people who say they are evangelicals. It is the well-understood world of Billy Graham, Pat Robertson, Jerry Falwell, Southern Baptists, Assemblies of God, and so much more; it is the realm of those who somehow place themselves inside it.[8] This culture is tremendously complex and diffuse, as I shall argue below. But as George Marsden points out, those diversities tend to pale in comparison with the outside world.[9] Neither its diversities nor its commonality can be forgotten in our discussions of evangelicalism, of course, but these days the doctrinal and cultural similarities most often get lost in scholarly discussions, just as the opposite seems true in the public press.

Other approaches may also prove promising. For example, there are those who think that what really counts in the mapping of religious groups are diverse images of religion, an idea whose time may well be coming.[10] Yet for now I propose to accept the definition derived from both beliefs and culture. By evangelicalism, I mean those people who operate in the publicly known evangelical and fundamentalist worlds, who see themselves as members of those worlds, and who usually believe in inerrant Scripture, assertive evangelization, and salvation through Jesus alone.

Defining the New Christian Right

More difficult, and by no means more securely rooted, will be my definition of the New Christian Right, a term wholly invented by the modern intellectual culture and the media, not at all indigenous to its adherents. One characteristic of the extensive literature on the New Christian Right is its lack of a uniform definition. Almost all this literature is grounded in public-attitude studies and shares their usual strengths and weaknesses. This literature does, however, sometimes contain important lessons, warning, for example, against the error of conflating the New Christian Right with all evangelicals or fundamentalists, or conflating the NCR with only evangelicals and fundamentalists.[11]

There is no reason to understand the New Christian Right in this fashion alone, noting areas of attitude agreement not only on social issues but also with respect to leaders and actions of the NCR. After all, what came to be called the New Christian Right has its own history, its own story, and is inseparable from any definition of it.[12] As I use the term, the New Christian Right will include those evangelicals and fundamentalists of the 1970s and 1980s who participated in or sympathized with the movement to bring conservative moral and social change to the United States, in line with their religious values.

What those values were and are is a subject of some disagreement, but also of some consensus.[13] I like Kenneth Wald's disposition to describe its social agenda as focused on family issues or, as the NCR put it, as "pro-family," including support for the traditional family, prayer and religion in the public schools, and sectarian religious education, and opposition to abortion, divorce, pornography, and the like.[14] At the same time, I strongly agree with Richard John Neuhaus's observation that participation in the decision-making process of the nation was also integral to the agenda.[15] These themes figured prominently among all sorts of social, economic, and foreign-policy ideas and positions held by such leaders of the movement as Falwell and Robertson.[16]

The Signs of Failure

Of course, measuring the impact of a movement is not an easy undertaking. There are bound to be methodological problems, and there are always definitional ones. How to measure impact and what counts as impact are permanent challenges. For me what counts in the end is policy success. I believe this was and is at the heart of the New Christian Right's effort. By this standard I don't see much success as yet and even less pending. More than anything else, I see failure.

This is clearly so if one looks, first, to institutional influence within the political system. Wherever we might cast our glance, the sight is not impressive from an NCR perspective. Some areas do not require much discussion. That the NCR got nowhere among the bureaucratic elites of the United States government is taken for granted today. Certainly no evidence has appeared to dispel this conclusion. In other arenas, such as interest groups, there are stories that began dramatically but have since fizzled. The most infamous example was the collapse of the Moral Majority.

This organizational demise cannot be dismissed lightly because the Moral Majority and Jerry Falwell came to stand, however inaccurately, for all of the NCR. Its members were going to remake America, realize the NCR agenda, and establish the NCR as a feared element in American politics. We know it did not work out that way. The fact that other NCR organizations are still in the field does not change either the real or the symbolic fate of the Moral Majority.[17]

Not only is the NCR's access to national bureaucracies limited, but its record in relation to the presidency is not impressive. Regular readers of the *Moral Majority Report* could not help but notice how frequently it bemoaned its lack of influence with the Reagan administration. The Bush era has hardly been more promising. Despite some symbolic bows, convention visits, and other pleasantries, precious little has been done in terms of a substantive legislative push toward the NCR social agenda.

Allen Hertzke's comparison of the NCR's record with that of Jewish groups at the White House is telling. Hertzke finds that shared religious disposition can be crucial in terms of access, and given the elite and mainline Protestant ambiance of the present White House, the NCR is at a tremendous disadvantage. Yet Jewish groups show this limitation need not be decisive if you insist on being heard, and have local and national organization that makes it politically essential that you be heard. The NCR lacks organization of that quality.[18]

Congress is no friendlier. Matthew Moen has argued that the NCR has played a role in agenda-setting there and in keeping its agenda highly visible. This is surely true regarding only one issue—abortion. And even on this issue coalition with some of the Catholics in and out of Congress has been essential. On other issues the NCR has not gotten anywhere in Congress. Nor is it likely to do so until there are far more members of Congress coming from its religious and cultural world. At the moment few indeed come from evangelical and fundamentalist churches, not to mention the NCR. Jesse Helms is an exception who proves the rule of NCR weakness in Congress.[19]

A stronger case can be made, perhaps, regarding the NCR's impact on the political-party system, though here, too, I wonder. Jerome Himmelstein argues, for example, that the NCR has succeeded in developing close connections to the Republican party, and this is a significant accomplishment.[20] But such a view begins by conceding that the NCR has utterly failed in the Democratic party. In fact, it has made no effort with that party at the national level, which is quite a concern given the Democrats' secure control of Congress and most statehouses.

Moreover, much discussion of the NCR's supposedly rising strength in Republican party circles notes both the increasing impact of NCR supporters and increasing divisiveness within the party resulting from their activities. Yet what the NCR seeks is change in the party's direction, not change that tears apart the only party vehicle in which it has any voice. Again, while much has been made of the appearance of NCR party activists in presidential races or, say, as delegates to the Republican state convention in Michigan, few tangible results are apparent after the shouting has subsided. Where are the victories within the Republican party, not to speak of the nation? They are not so obvious, though the legacy of nasty intra-party fights is.[21]

Public Opinion and Policy

We might choose, then, to go another route and look at the war for public opinion and, along with that, for signs of electoral impact. Although it is not now succeeding in governmental institutions, perhaps the NCR will make progress with the public and at the polls. There are a few signs of good news here for the NCR, but the overwhelming tale is one of defeat.

Despite grandiose claims and alarm in some circles, the NCR does not have a particular record of success in its public-opinion and electoral endeavors, certainly not after 1980, and, arguably, not even then. Yes, it ran a candidate for president, but he lost badly in the Republican primaries in 1988. And though considerable evidence shows cohesive voting by NCR supporters, and evangelicals and fundamentalists in general, for Republican candidates for president in the 1980s,[22] Kenneth Wald has looked at that evidence, and his conclusion is noteworthy for its skepticism about the NCR and its electoral effects. He is not impressed with its cohesion and observes that it was mostly Republican, at least in presidential voting, before the movement began. A good deal of its Republican presidential voting can, moreover, be attributed to other factors, including the manifest popularity of Ronald Reagan.[23]

Robert Wuthnow's conclusion seems undeniable. The NCR simply lost the battle for public opinion in the 1980s.[24] This was particularly painful as there was and is a good deal of support for many of its social-issue positions. Yet when the New Christian Right organized and became publicly active, the general public gave it low ratings. This situation was illustrated most famously by the public disgust expressed toward the tremendously unpopular Moral Majority.[25]

The televangelists and the campaign against them also played a role, of course, in undercutting public support and electoral impact. Wild exaggerations of media influence (later discovered to be inaccurate) were followed by the denouncement of Jim Bakker. These charges effectively discredited the televangelists among the larger public, an accomplishment long sought by every opponent of the NCR. Here again was no NCR success story.[26]

Finally, there can be no avoiding the bottom line—the record on policy. Wald says it as it is: "For the most part, the record has been one of failure."[27] Has the central NCR agenda seen any significant advancement on the national or, indeed, on many state levels? No. Has the family been strengthened the way the NCR envisioned? Has prayer entered the public schools, the movement toward gay rights been turned back, pornography been seriously attacked, or the Constitution amended regarding abortion? The answer to these questions is no. Even on abortion, where the record is best, the NCR is reduced to the old strategy, once contemptible in its eyes, of depending on the Supreme Court to do its work for it as public opinion slowly turns more and more "pro-choice."

Other Readings

There is nothing self-evident about my argument. Though some agree with me,[28] other observers offer more favorable readings. But I want to suggest why some distance from these favorable readings may be appropriate.

A good many students of this subject are deeply impressed with the accomplishments of the NCR and would reject any description of it as a failure. My focus here is not on the hysterical analysts who let loose a decade or so ago; they have long since moved on to other, more exciting arenas. My attention is on serious students who urge us to look in many directions.

Hubert Morken has done some excellent work on NCR activity in a number of local settings, and he finds that the NCR is far from dead. I agree with him. But local activity here and there should not be taken by anyone as a sign of much strength. It must be put in context, and that context is an overall miserable job by NCR organizations to build and wield power at local levels.[29]

Craig Bledsoe, in his thoughtful reflection on NCR politics after the Moral Majority, sees a suitably mixed picture. It is hard to disagree. But his analysis singles out the legal world as a particular place of advance for the NCR. Though there has been some movement toward using litigation and constructing the legal infra-structure for litigation, however, conservative Christians today are simply not yet in the big leagues in legal/judicial politics.[30]

Of course, the entire story of the NCR cannot be told by describing only the fate of the Moral Majority. Lots of other organizations are busy, and much goes on at the local level that cannot be ignored. Concerned Women for America, the Family Research Council, the Religious Roundtable, and the like proceed, but the reality is that they are diffuse and have no deep impact. The absence of policy accomplishments, aside from something like the equal-access bill in which they played a modest role, is manifest.[31]

Let me acknowledge that the idea that the NCR has mobilized over the past decade quite a few men and women into political activity may well have something to it. A good deal of energy has entered the system through the Republican party, from the elite to the mass level. Pat Robertson has run for president, and, probably more significantly, a good many evangelicals and fundamentalists have become Republicans. This reality is undeniable, and it constitutes a measurable impact.

It is fair to speculate that the NCR movement is responsible for many changes,[32] but it is not responsible for all. As Lyman Kellstedt and Mark Noll remark in their longitudinal study of evangelical presidential voting since 1948, the Republican realignment of the 1980s had decidedly begun before the emergence of the New Christian Right.[33] From a less technical and broader perspective, I do not see any larger effects, certainly not in policy terms, nor even, in the Bush era, in terms of the directions of the Republican party. Things may be different in the future, of course.

Reasons for Optimism?

A more cautious soul might suggest that, while the evidence of great effect is slim, we are in mid-journey. From this perspective, it is just much too early to assess consequences, including institutional or policy consequences. I like this slant a good deal, and it may be right. For instance, there is something to Jeffrey Hadden's point that, as overblown as were many early analyses of political televangelism's reach, a tremendous capacity still remains in place: an elaborate broadcast organization, money connected with it (though much less than there was just a few years ago), an aging population, and other factors. Opportunity is not gone.[34] Consider, too, all the struggling NCR organizations. How much do we really know about them? How much do we understand about them as possible seed-planters for the future? There are a lot of unanswered questions, some because the research is not done, some because not enough time has passed. Yet a good deal of the uncertainty revolves around what might happen in the future, an obviously elusive realm. We can cheerfully grant that all sorts of things might happen without undermining my argument that the NCR has just not gotten very far yet.

Still another perspective takes us back to another part of the

NCR agenda. From a vantage point outside NCR circles (though sometimes also reflected within), what matters is the increase of participation that the NCR has facilitated for a considerable group of people in our nation. Put more directly, some argue that from the view of democratic theory the NCR is a success of sorts. It aimed to bring new people into the system, and it has. Some of these people may be angry, some not, but they are there now. Was this not, as Richard John Neuhaus argued, what the fundamentalists really wanted?[35]

As I have suggested, though some laud this result, within the confines of liberal intellectual opinion it is distinctly less popular. In such circles concern over the perceived danger of the NCR outweighed and outweighs the suggestion that the NCR's existence has contributed to democracy in the United States.

Looking at the same phenomenon somewhat differently, one might conclude that the religious worlds upon which the NCR has drawn are being increasingly integrated into the larger culture. Again, not everyone approves. This reality garners no praise from really militant separatist fundamentalists, or from secularists who also have little use for religious culture. Neither group sees cause for celebration in the evidence that liberal culture and its engines are swallowing all.[36]

Whenever I encounter Cal Thomas's newspaper column in my hometown newspaper—my hometown being a city whose cultural tone is both very liberal and noticeably secular—I appreciate the argument that the NCR and its allies did get somewhere in terms of representation. They did re-enter the public square, and they are there now with all the others.

Yet I confess to some skepticism. I need to see more evidence that the NCR penetrated American political and policy-making institutions before I am convinced that they got much in terms of representation. Representation does not mean tokenism. Representation means being taken seriously, in a positive way, and actually getting somewhere. It is not about always winning, but it is about winning more than the NCR did. I wonder how many citizens want representation just for the record. The success of the NCR, as an illustration of democratic representation, turns in good part on how successful it has been in seeing its agenda become policy.

Merely being on the agenda amounts to little if the outcome of the "culture war" is defeat.[37]

Reflections Toward Explanation

If New Christian Right success is mostly an illusion, the appropriate query is why. I want to argue that the reasons are complex. There is no easy answer to why the NCR did not do better. Thus there is no quick fix that can be suggested to those, of whatever political persuasion within the evangelical and fundamentalist world, who endeavor to learn from the situation of the NCR as they face the future. At the same time, I want to cut through the tangle of reasons and conundrums to pinpoint two implacable barriers that doomed the NCR and promise the same fate for any of its successors.

Division in the ranks was a crucial factor in the stumbling of the NCR. To begin with, the very nature of the evangelical and fundamentalist communities created problems. Evangelicals differed in terms of history, theology, and racial background, to name three crucial variables. The many cultures and attitudes that exist within the evangelical and fundamentalist world lead in no single direction, just as Jerry Falwell, Billy Graham, Beverly LeHaye, Pat Robertson, and John Perkins are five very different folks.[38]

The truth is that the NCR acquired the aura in many evangelical circles of a movement of fundamentalists, and I think this hurt it among those not identifying with fundamentalists. Jerry Falwell made this judgment himself, and it is why he eventually tried so hard to appeal to evangelicals. He saw a weak flank, but he was not able to protect himself.[39]

Also significant were basic theological or political divisions over the legitimacy of cultural involvement in general, and political action specifically. Often related were disagreements over the appropriate degree of separation of church and state. The shadings within the ranks of evangelical and fundamentalist religion on these matters are often of exquisite degree, and each degree can make a great deal of difference.

In seeking to enter the field of politics, the NCR broke with a perceived traditional mold. That the historical record revealed considerable evangelical political activity was beside the point. The impression inside and outside evangelical and fundamentalist circles was that the NCR was innovative, both theologically and practically, on the issue of political involvement. This did not sit well with many, especially those in the Bob Jones wing of fundamentalists who strenuously advocated cultural and political separatism. The fear remained that the losers in such an enterprise might be the fundamentalists, if the larger culture was transforming rather than transformed. Paradoxically, the separatist fundamentalist Christian school movement gained momentum at the same time as did those urging political engagement in the larger culture.

While "respectable" participation in politics, like voting, was very much acceptable within evangelicalism, aggressive political action connected with religious concerns clearly made many evangelicals —and some fundamentalists, too—uneasy, especially those for whom the traditional concept of separation of church and state was sincerely honored. Again, it was no accident that Jerry Falwell found himself busy reassuring evangelicals and fundamentalists that he was just as committed to that separation as they were.[40]

Something of a middle way received the approval of the ever-respectable *Christianity Today* and of such admired models as Senator Mark Hatfield, the evangelical senator from Oregon, and Charles Colson, the reformed Nixon operative. For them, the NCR was both too political and not political enough. On the one hand, it was too devoted to flag-waving cultural nationalism and, on the other hand, too unrepentant in its cultural separatism.[41]

Perhaps the NCR's biggest disappointment was Billy Graham's studied distance. He had long bewailed the cultural corruption of the United States and had no serious record of advocating cultural separatism. Indeed, Graham had a lengthy history of consorting with top-level politicians, from Eisenhower to Ford, in a public fashion. Yet it is clear that the NCR was too sectarian for this non-sectarian evangelist, and he seemed to sign off with sober warnings about the danger of civil religion and the collapse of the venerable church-state distinction.[42]

Then there were the divisions over issues and candidates. Though some of these had theological bases, they could often be read as cultural in origin, as, for example, the evangelical reluctance to support the Pentecostal fundamentalist Pat Robertson. In practice, theology and culture can be difficult to separate as motivations, and they certainly were in this instance.

A third dimension of the NCR's problems was the genuine disagreement over political issues within the laity. Even the membership of the Moral Majority, after all, was marked by diversity beyond its set of social issues. In fact, except on social issues, no political consensus existed within the "community" the NCR sought to mobilize. Thus it was hard to mobilize even those willing to accept the religious legitimacy of strong political action. There simply was no monolith waiting to receive its marching orders.[43]

To these divisions in the ranks, by now well understood, one last may be added that requires a specific emphasis it rarely receives. Though data on issues and voting indicate no particular division between evangelicals and fundamentalists, one definitely prevails between more than a few oft-published, articulate evangelical voices (should I say elites?) and the NCR.

Many evangelical religious and intellectual leaders clearly disassociated themselves from the Moral Majority and the broader NCR, quickly and firmly. I believe it hurt that movement from every possible angle. Usually citing intellectual reasons for their disassociation, these leaders harshly criticized fundamentalist theology, politics, style of politics, or understanding of American history, among other things.[44] But this was not the entire story. In my work and association with evangelical intellectuals and clergy, I continue to be impressed by the depth of their hostility toward fundamentalism. Anything connected with fundamentalism, as the NCR is, may expect the same fate. The evidence suggests that these feelings are sometimes intellectual and theological in origin; sometimes they are a reflection of the larger culture's opinions; sometimes they are related to the personal journeys of their articulators. In any case, there is no doubt that evangelical-elite hostility toward the NCR was a factor, a division in the ranks, that should not be dismissed.

Operational Problems

In his 1990 remarks to the founding meeting of the Christian Coalition, an NCR organization, Paul Weyrich made much of the operational problems of the NCR as he tried to explain why it failed so decisively.[45]

Weyrich is far from the only observer to give so much weight to this factor. In a broad sense, what was important for the NCR was the vexing matter of playing politics—how to do that successfully without imitating the political culture of self-interest and pragmatic advantage. Among the problems were the need to learn how to think strategically and understand how the political game is played; to develop a core of trained people who knew these rules and could educate others; to be tough enough to take on controversy when it was advantageous (and not withdraw at the first bad-weather flag); to be careful about too much "niceness," resisting co-optation when possible; and to be willing to build coalitions whenever worthwhile, even in the face of what Allen Hertzke calls "the bewildering diversity and theological differences in the evangelical world."[46]

On each of these points, the record was mixed. The real issue was how good the NCR's strategic judgment was in practice. There was at first a distaste for, and an expressed superiority to, politics; there was a great deal of discomfort about forming coalitions outside the evangelical-fundamentalist world, and plenty of difficulty in doing so within it. On many policy issues, including abortion, and on politicians, particularly Pat Robertson and George Bush, there was confusion about whether to compromise and build coalitions or not. But how much this was just a matter of learning for the new kid on the block and thus perfectly natural, and how much it reflected intractable structural problems, including the deep divisions within the ranks, remains open for debate.[47]

Also significant were such basic factors as money, leadership, and the role of the televangelists. Despite some well-publicized claims by the secular media, the truth is that the NCR was hobbled by a lack of financial resources. Much was apparently squandered by competing causes and organizations, while efforts to raise funds for political activity proved disappointing.[48]

And there is the question of leadership. We don't yet have the perspective to evaluate Falwell, Robertson, and others within the NCR in terms of their abilities as leaders. I would hazard the claim, though, that in the end their strength proved to be their weakness.

Masters of publicity, they did not know how to move from television to the streets or the corridors of Congress. Like ineffective evangelists, they generated publicity, but in a hostile environment, rather than acquiring the savvy and building the tight organizations that were needed once the hoopla was over.

Lastly, the televangelist scandals created a terrible operational mess. They brought great discredit to the NCR and provided a wonderful opening for attack by the NCR's enemies.[49] They proved especially embarrassing for mainstream evangelicals and further exacerbated the internal divisions within evangelicalism.[50] Yet the televangelist scandals were an almost predictable result of larger structural dynamics, above all the pluralistic and individualistic character of evangelical and fundamentalist religion, in theory and in practice. Again and again, structural problems lay beneath the NCR's operational follies.

The Other Culture

On top of all these problems, the NCR failed because it faced a culture that was on the whole not sympathetic and sometimes distinctly hostile. Robert Wuthnow argues that most people who were alert to the cultural conflict between the NCR and its left-liberal opponents were not especially sympathetic to either view.[51] No doubt he is right. The greatest challenge for the NCR was the reality of pluralism in the modern United States. Our culture is arguably more pluralistic than at any time in its history. The most relevant expression of this pluralism may be the seemingly endless variety of lifestyles and values.[52] In the face of such variety, the NCR and its constituency discovered the truth that they were just one group, and a rather fractious one at that.

And yet pluralism does not mean anarchy in belief structure (though how far away that condition is constitutes a serious question). The text of cultural consensus may be brief, but it is not altogether missing. One of its main chapters remains commitment to church-state separatism. While this principle is not particularly honored in practice, it has its ideological power in our pluralistic culture. Undoubtedly, this belief stands as a barrier to the NCR, given the widespread suspicion that the New Christian Right wishes to impose a particular theocracy on a diverse and freedom-loving society.[53]

But we need a tough and realistic power analysis as a supplement here. We need to talk about those who have power in this society and ask about the balance. In particular, we need to ask about political and cultural elites. Allen Hertzke maintains that access is crucial to power in the interest-group/congressional nexus of Washington. How to obtain access is, of course, complicated, as it always has been. But Hertzke argues that, in many issue areas of religion and politics, ideological agreement or sympathy between lobbyists and their targets is vital.[54]

What this means is that the NCR had great difficulty being heard in Washington. Few members of Congress were part of the NCR, and not many evangelicals and fundamentalists were there either. Moreover, I know of no one who has any evidence suggesting that upper levels of government outside of Congress were honeycombed with NCR sympathizers, or any kind of religiously conservative Christians.[55] And, as the NCR itself has repeatedly claimed, pleasant public visits to the White House produced very little.

Studies of ideological congruence and religious activism have a long way to go. We know too little about the religious ideology of members of Congress, not to speak of other powerful members of our national government (or state and local governments). We know more about the relationship between the NCR and the cultural elites involved in setting and interpreting values in our society. Crucial portions of this latter group, we know, are generally indifferent to religion and are socially liberal. In short, we know that this sector had at the outset no ideological sympathy for the NCR.[56]

Predispositions, moreover, were not the whole story. They turned into action. The decade of the 1980s saw repeated assaults on the NCR, by, among others, the elite media. In the media the NCR encountered a major impediment. Tina Rosenberg's study, which once seemed bold, is no longer disputed. The elite media in a real sense "made" the Moral Majority—in our broader terms, the NCR—through their extensive coverage and often flamboyant denunciations.[57] I am not aware of any data yet establishing that the media also "unmade" the NCR, but I suspect that they did hurt the NCR in the popular mind. Aided by the NCR's own errors, the media's hostility may explain why even those citizens who shared the Moral Majority's policy positions offered it only limited support.[58] Overwhelming evidence of the furious assault on the NCR, which Rosenberg noted, is available to any reader or listener. *Time* magazine is a good example of modern Manhattan secularism at its most militant, and *Time* struck every blow it could at the New Christian Right.[59]

The only perceptible change now is that the NCR no longer constitutes "news"; that is, it is no longer threatening. But the attack went on elsewhere and still does. What we may call overall "the liberal reaction" was very negative.[60] The attitude of other Protestants should not be underestimated. Here I refer to the role that elite non-evangelical Protestant voices lent to the critique.

Liberal Protestants were in the forefront. *Christian Century* systematically gave an outlet to critics. Harvey Cox blasted fundamentalist political dispositions, and, of great significance, Martin Marty added his judgment that fundamentalism gave rise to a simplistic and backward perspective and unacceptable politics. While it intrigued both Cox and Marty that such a reactionary outlook made such good use of modern technology, it did not lead them to revise their judgment of the movement as a whole.[61]

There were other views, of course, that tried to get away from sensational charges and emotive claims, applying instead sober analysis and sometimes even sympathetic reflection. Perhaps the most important was Neuhaus's understanding portrayal of the purposes of the NCR.[62] But it is not obvious they had much effect in the larger debate. For despite these more balanced opinions, the American public clearly judged the NCR very negatively very soon after it appeared on the political scene.

Lessons Learned

In conclusion, I want to explore whether the NCR and its evangelical and fundamentalist allies really have a political future. In my view, some things can be learned and overcome; some cannot. Experience can change a lot of amateur behavior in any activity, including politics, and I believe the operational errors made by the NCR are not inherent or irretrievable in the long run. But how can the intense divisions in the ranks of theologically conservative Protestantism be changed? After all, at this very moment, we see indications of a massive and historic split in the Southern Baptist Convention.

Historical, theological, and political divisions are very strong. They conquered the NCR just as they would any other political movement, whatever its orientation, that sought to build from disparate worlds. Sectarianism is not the story of leftist political history only.

And how can such political movements deal with the animosity of governmental, media, and cultural-religious elites within the country? In a sense, the NCR was founded on the discovery that conservative religious hegemony was very much lost in the elite circles of the United States. The battles that followed in the 1980s only confirmed this reality. The barn door, in short, proved to be shut fairly tightly.

This conclusion does not mean that the NCR is dead. Nor does it mean that other political movements, with different orientations, will not arise from within evangelicalism in the years ahead. Perhaps the NCR has pioneered the acceptability of such efforts for the future. What it does mean, as I estimate the situation, is that the expectations of their proponents and the fears of their opponents should be low. These new kids on the block are not likely to be beating up much of anyone.

Response

Carl F. H. Henry

UNDER a republican form of government, politics necessarily becomes an arena of civic compromise in ordering public affairs. Few devout Christians expect statute law in this context to inaugurate the Kingdom of God. If the New Christian Right entertained any such expectation, it was clearly misled. But the contrary verdict that the New Christian Right was an absolute failure may well be excessive. Insofar as it proclaimed and promoted some legitimate concerns in an authentically Christian way, positive achievements accrued to it. For biblically grounded Christians the measure of success, after all, is finally to be found not in world triumph but in spiritual obedience to God in all realms of activity.

To its credit, the New Christian Right established the evangelical community as a politically identifiable force in a generation when an ecumenical Protestant-Catholic-Jewish alliance had virtually nullified its public importance. The NCR advanced beyond my plea in *The Uneasy Conscience of Modern Fundamentalism* (1947) that evangelicals re-enter the cultural arena to press the claims of the biblical world-and-life view comprehensively upon modern society. The NCR sponsored a political movement promoting specific legislation compatible with Christian values. It did so to counter civic government's increasing intrusion into church-state concerns, most notably by restriction of prayer in public schools and by federal funding of abortion. The NCR placed the discussion of moral values conspicuously and ongoingly on the agenda of American political life at a time when secular society tended to reduce to merely private concerns the public relevance of both morality and religion.

Carl F. H. Henry, one of America's leading evangelical theologians, is the author of over thirty-five books on theology, ethics, and evangelical social thought, including *The Uneasy Conscience of Modern Fundamentalism*.

The importance of these achievements would seem clear in an era when many office-holders are more concerned with whether it any longer "pays" to oppose abortion or some other evil than they are with whether a given policy is right or wrong. These achievements were, nonetheless, gained at a considerable price. Fowler ably analyzes much of the toll. If one were to expand his list of complaints, one might note that in several respects the NCR was as much influenced by—rather than being an influence upon—the very culture it sought to transform.

For one thing some conservatives, long withdrawn from cultural concerns, now returned with exaggerated expectations from political engagement, and minimized the role of evangelical proclamation. The initially announced aim was to restore America to Christian moorings by legislation. Even more disconcerting was the political methodology, which reflected the emotive rather than the rational character of contemporary politics. Reasoned discourse was neglected for semantic combat. Media one-liners compensated for a lack of think tanks, and public demonstration largely replaced the effort to persuade wavering or unconvinced office-holders. Extensive mail solicitation of funds at times took on a melodramatic and histrionic character. In short, the NCR largely forfeited the opportunity to formulate a persuasive public philosophy and to exhibit what it means to engage in politics Christianly, while it relied on the methodology of secular politics and of the secular media in the effort to lift secular politics to a new plateau.

Without summarizing the imposing list of complaints Fowler adduces, and which here and there one might wish to nuance somewhat, I would like to expand on his closing concession: that the NCR is not yet deceased, and that other somewhat similar and even more refined movements may arise within evangelicalism, even if Fowler himself thinks contemporary society will have little to fear from them. There can be little doubt that the momentum of the NCR has slowed, and evangelical political engagement lacks cohesiveness and leadership. Strident and conflicting evangelical voices sometimes manifest little more civility in public dialogue than does the McLaughlin Group on television. The vivid contrasts extend from the Christian Reconstructionists, whose verbal assaults on those who differ encourage some to wonder whether they would rather take their chances of survival in a radically Shiite society than in one run by some Christian theonomists, to those whose main interest is merely in some single issue and not at all in a canopy view of the political order.

Yet Thomas C. Atwood, the former controller of the exploratory committee for Pat Robertson's campaign for the Republican presidential nomination, thinks the critical question is not whether the NCR has a future but whether its continuing influence—given the accelerating decline of humanistic culture—will be best preserved by cultural isolation as an ideologically pure voice, or by venturing a coalition consensus ("Through a Glass Darkly," *Policy Review*, no. 54 [Fall 1990]: 44–52). Atwood views the recent setbacks as temporary and transitional to making a larger impact at state and local levels, involving a co-belligerency that emphasizes shared concerns and values more than religious identification. Atwood, who is managing editor of *Policy Review*, thinks the Evangelical Right can overcome the earlier isolation that limited its cultural leadership roles, and transcend an exclusion from public influence to which the so-called intellectual elite's bigotry against religious conservatives contributed. Atwood emphasizes the readiness of the NCR to learn from the mistakes of its recent past. Much current evangelical literature accordingly stresses the need for cognitive modesty, principled compromise, servant-leadership, consensus-building predicated on general revelation rather than a particular religious metaphysics, and constructively affirming the authority (albeit limited) of government.

If evangelicals can avoid overstating their strength and entrepreneurial candidates can escape from premature efforts to capitalize politically on the evangelical thrust, if they can learn not to attribute to politics an absolutism more appropriate to religious doctrine and avoid making political loyalties a test of orthodoxy, if they can view political engagement as a means of serving rather than dominating society—and these are imposing "ifs"—Atwood thinks that in the near future Christian citizenship will be significantly enhanced and accelerated. Jerry Falwell's Moral Majority and Pat Robertson's presidential campaign would be the grains of wheat from which developed an enlivened Christian citizenship and a stimulus that, stripped of its flaws, may yet yield a new cadre of Christian leaders in the public arena.

Comments

A. JAMES REICHLEY: Robert Booth Fowler makes a strong and somewhat convincing case about the political effectiveness of the New Religious Right in the 1980s. But the whole question is something like the argument about whether a Republican president could check domestic spending in the 1980s.

Both in government policy and in the moral direction of the country, there were trends in the 1960s and 1970s that, projected outward, would have taken us to a far different place than we are today. Fowler is right that the New Religious Right didn't change the direction of the country, but it did check some of the trends that were under way. That was a negative achievement, and a modest one in terms of the movement's aspirations.

PAUL WEYRICH: The Christian Right learned several lessons in the 1980s.

First, it learned that there is no political savior. For people who profess Christianity, of course, it is extraordinary that there was ever the thought of a possible political savior. Some of our people forgot what they believed in theologically, and they waited for a political savior to come in and take care of all these problems. They have become wiser now and know that there is no such political savior; there isn't going to be one; and anything that is achieved is going to have to be achieved incrementally and not by some magical force.

Second, the New Religious Right now understands the importance of being involved locally. Fowler minimized that, suggesting that it was much more impressive that the Religious New Right was involved at the national level, and many of you weren't sure that being involved at the local level was victory. I call it victory precisely because, as both Mayor Daley and Tip O'Neill said, "All politics is local politics." You can't run a successful national political movement without a local base. You could elect Jesse Helms president, and he wouldn't be able to make any progress on the social

78

agenda or any other agenda if the political apparatus of the country was controlled entirely by the opposition. . . .

Go with my friend Ralph Reed to some of the meetings he has around the country. Go with the Focus on the Family people. Take a look at the mechanics of the Southern Baptist operation, which is now in conservative hands. These are not accomplishments to be minimalized. These are large organizations with lots of resources and with rather able people at the top. Take a look at this kind of activity. Compared to the rallies of ten years ago, it is far more significant, far more sophisticated, and, I think, will yield far greater results—provided we can come up with leadership able to take advantage of it. . . .

Another thing supporters of the movement learned is that, in a battle for the common good, they must make alliances with other people and talk with other people who are not precisely who or what they are. I think great progress has been made in this regard, but one stumbling block remains. Christians in politics still seem to think, wrongly, that they have to give up their point of view. Christians are such nice people that they're ill-equipped to fight the kind of battles they've been involved in.

This was the problem with the movement's arrival on the national scene. Its ill-equipped leaders didn't have a clear agenda, didn't go through the political process, didn't know what they were doing, and had no concept of how to win or even of how to get from A to B. All of a sudden these people were on the national scene, and of course they made every stupid statement imaginable. It's not surprising that certain people's negatives went way up. If I were a neutral observer, not knowing these people and not convinced they were trying to do good, I would have watched them and said to myself, "what stupid idiots." A lot of people did say that because, in the political realm, a lot of our leaders were stupid.

Our biggest weakness is still our lack of a national leadership that is as determined as, for example, the civil-rights leadership is to fight for its agenda on the national level. We have nothing comparable. Moreover, if you suggested to most of the people in this movement that they would have to play the level of hardball that the civil-rights leadership does, they would be distraught. It's just not quite in their character. I don't know whether they can develop that thick-skinned determination or not, but they need it for the movement to achieve a far greater potential than it had in the last ten years. . . .

Finally, I want to say something about the supposed destruction of the movement by the media. This movement was *not* a media-created operation. Indeed, the media was angry because it took them several years to discover what had already been built. When they discovered it in 1980, its political agenda was so far advanced that the media started wondering, "Who are these people? What are they doing here?"

The fury with which the media reported on the movement had a lot to do with embarrassment at their own ignorance. Editors were being fired all over the place because they were supposed to know about major political movements, and, in this case, they were behind the curve. So I deny categorically that the New Religious Right was a media-created movement. It was there before the media got to it. And though the media and the cultural elites are clearly hostile to the movement, that is not necessarily a liability if we can develop a leadership that knows how to handle them.

TERRY EASTLAND: At what point did the Religious Right get involved in the political system? Whether it understood the nature of separation of powers, federalism, and the American Constitution or not, it got involved at a natural point of entry, namely the American presidency. For better or worse, the American presidency is the most complicated and interesting of the three branches of the national government, and, intuitively, anyone in the country would think that it is the place to go to get things changed. A succession of presidents from F.D.R. on down, and even before that, has given Americans the idea that this is where to go to try to affect the political system. It is not a bad judgment because the presidency has enormous discretionary power and, under the Constitution, the power to appoint the federal judiciary.

In 1987 Ronald Reagan nominated three different individuals in order to get one person he wanted on the Supreme Court. And contrary to some claims, the actual text of the Constitution was very important in giving the president the upper hand. The sheer power to appoint allowed President Reagan to continue to nominate until he got a person that, on balance, gave him about 80 per cent of the jurisprudence he wanted. Not bad.

I think it is important to understand the impact of the Religious Right upon presidential elections and the formal powers of office. I would encourage anyone to look at the judiciary. President Reagan appointed 372 judges, who comprise more than half of the sitting federal judiciary. It is a little-known fact about American politics that today the president nominates a judge every eight days on average. This is an extraordinary number—and the fact suggests his extraordinary power.

Another area of executive power that journalists and academics often overlook is the power of the president to litigate in the courts through the solicitor general. If you both appoint justices to the Supreme Court and shape the arguments that you give to the justices, you can use two branches of the government to get results. This is an important dynamic that political scientists undervalue.

RALPH REED: I would not dispute many of the points in Robert Booth Fowler's paper. He is correct about White House tokenism, the few inroads made in Congress, lack of significant public-policy victories (yet), and the long distance that is left to go. But it is important to realize that we are, in historical terms, still in the infancy of a political movement that I believe will have a long and distinguished future.

As someone who has spent time studying such movements, I'd like to call attention to the example of the National Association for the Advancement of Colored People (NAACP), which was founded in 1909. If the NAACP had held a conference as late as 1939, its members would have said that the organization was a failure. All it had gained in thirty years was tokenism from Eleanor Roosevelt and some support from elements within the Democratic party. No significant civil-rights bill had been passed, and a federal anti-lynching law had been possibly its best victory. Not until 1947 was there a civil-rights platform in one of the two major political parties. The *Brown* v. *Board of Education* decision did not come down until 1954; a civil-rights bill did not get through the Congress until 1957. Not until 1964 or 1965 did the classic anti-segregation, pro-integration civil-rights struggle finally come to fruition at the national level.

I would suggest that *Webster* might be our *Brown* v. *Board*. It may be a little too early to tell what is going to happen, but I think *Webster* will return the battleground to the fifty states. Fifty battles will be going on, with each taking on its own shape. Our case is similar to that of the anti-saloon and temperance movement, which really began in the 1830s and 1840s and resulted in a patchwork of laws that led to Prohibition. By the time the Prohibition Amendment was ratified in 1919, three-quarters of the states were already dry. This is what I see *Webster* doing. It will force us to go back and do what every great social and political movement has had to do: win at the national level by winning first at the state, county, and precinct levels.

I anticipate two trends in the future. First, autonomous and semi-autonomous state and local organizations will be built up to fight and win state and local battles. The movements that will prosper in the next ten or twenty years will be those that set up organizations in conjunction with precinct captains, county coordinators, congressional district coordinators, and others to emulate the way we elect and defeat people. Second, training will play a major role. We have held thirteen or fourteen two-day training seminars designed to teach the nuts and bolts of political action: how to win elections; how to deal with the media; how to raise money; and how to organize, recruit, and speak as a candidate.

These two phenomena bode well for the future. A grass-roots movement will operate through many local organizations with the aid of cadres of trained, technically proficient activists. Together they will win victories—which seems like a very bright future to me.

ROBERT DUGAN: I am often asked: why do evangelicals align themselves so much with the Republican party? The reverse may be even more the case. The Republican party aligns itself with evangelicals because, as Paul Weyrich and many others have observed, evangelicals are more conservative, generally, than are most other segments of the population. Republicans have been actively cultivating evangelicals, and the Republican party was a natural place for them to end up.

I could document a series of meetings from 1979 on that would show the inclinations of the Republican party with respect to evangelicals. The National Association of Evangelicals (NAE) was asked in 1984 if it would like to testify before the Republican party's platform committee. We accepted. We made plans months in advance and testified, but we also took the initiative and went to the Democrats when we realized that the Democrats were not going to come to us for their platform committee. The NAE is not part of a particular political organization. We can't be, and we are not. Our people are in both parties. We are anxious to have our input anywhere we can.

In response to our overture, a Democratic staffer told us that the Democrats were not going to have such hearings. He lied. The Democratic party platform committee held public hearings in Kansas City on May 31 and in Columbus, Ohio, four days later. The National Abortion Rights Action League (NARAL) was invited, but the NAE was not. I asked if we could submit written testimony. The staffer who responded said, with clear boredom in his voice, "Yes, well, if you get testimony in to us." When I then asked about the deadline and the number of copies he would need, he answered that two copies would be plenty, even though I can't imagine that they would pull the staple and use their Xerox machine. They did not even pretend to be interested.

You have a party, then, with a gay and lesbian caucus since 1984, that at least unofficially has antagonized evangelicals. You have another party that has cultivated evangelicals and tailored its platform to suit our moral concerns. Given this state of affairs, it is not surprising that evangelicals identify more with Republicans. This may not be ideal, but it is the way things are because the Republicans have been cultivating us for over a decade.

RICHARD D. LAND: I think the biggest failure of the movement we've been analyzing is typified by the pigmentation of the people around this table. There is no way the evangelically aligned movement can really change our culture unless it can expand from being a largely white movement. It's not primarily a middle-class movement; it's a lower middle-class, working-class, and blue-collar movement. But it has not made common cause with African-Americans and Hispanics. Several reasons account for this, not the least of which is the fact that Sunday morning is still the most segregated moment in American life.

The people who have been wronged are not going to assume we want to work with them unless we make it clear by taking the initiative and reaching out to them in demonstrable and repeated ways. In the case of African-Americans, in particular, we must go to their leadership, who seem far more wedded to the Democratic party than the Evangelical Right has ever been to the Republican party. It seems to me that we share with African-American churches and with Hispanic culture a lot of common ground on what we would call traditional-values issues. This outreach should be one of the highest priorities of evangelicals in the last decade of the twentieth century. Demographics tell us, if nothing else does, that we're diminishing our potential to have any kind of base if we don't do this.

DONALD WILDMON: The New Christian Right will be around for a long time. I keep hearing the terms "winning" and "losing," and I must confess that I would like to win. But there is something higher that the secular mind does not understand. In the final analysis, winning or losing is not the ultimate issue. The ultimate issue is that those involved be faithful. Whether we succeed or not is not entirely in our hands. Our job is to be faithful.

A. James Reichley is a senior fellow at the Brookings Institution; **Paul Weyrich** is president of the Free Congress Foundation; **Terry Eastland** is a resident fellow at the Ethics and Public Policy Center; **Ralph Reed** is executive director of the Christian Coalition; **Robert Dugan** is director of public affairs, National Association of Evangelicals; **Richard D. Land** is director of the Christian Life Commission of the Southern Baptist Convention; and **Donald Wildmon** is president of the American Family Association.

4

Evangelical Voting Patterns:
1976–1988

Corwin Smidt

THE purpose of this essay is threefold: (1) to probe the nature of the contemporary American evangelical political involvement and assess its political significance, (2) to analyze the relationship between the evangelical community and the New Religious Right, and (3) to assess the potential of the New Religious Right to draw support from segments of the black community, particularly from among black evangelical voters. To accomplish these tasks, I will analyze national public-opinion surveys. Given that most national surveys prior to 1976 contained few religious questions beyond denominational affiliation and church attendance, the analysis is confined largely to social and political changes evident among evangelicals over the course of the presidential elections of 1976, 1980, 1984, and 1988.

My thesis is that changes in the 1980s among both evangelicals and members of the New Religious Right have significant political implications. Evangelicals have grown in political importance; mass support for the organizational bases of the New Religious Right has waned, and, as a result, its base of support has become

Corwin Smidt is professor of political science at Calvin College in Michigan. He has published numerous articles on the topics of political socialization, voting behavior, and religion and politics.

increasingly tied to the evangelical community; and opportunities exist for the New Religious Right to expand its base within portions of the black community, particularly among black evangelicals.

Attempting to substantiate these contentions through the analysis of survey data poses various problems. While not unusual ones, these problems should be addressed so that readers will be better able to evaluate my arguments.

The Definition of Evangelicals

At the outset, it should be noted that how one defines the word "evangelical" has important consequences, for the nature of one's findings can be significantly affected by the particular definition one employs. For example, some argue that those Roman Catholics who exhibit an evangelical style of religious behavior should be classified as evangelicals,[1] whereas others claim that one should exclude Roman Catholics from the ranks of American evangelicals.[2] Even if all agreed that only certain Protestants should be labeled as evangelicals, other definitional issues remain. For example, are evangelicals best viewed as members of particular denominations (outside the realm of "mainline" Protestant denominations), or as individuals who subscribe to certain doctrinal essentials, regardless of denominational affiliation? Moreover, the nature of one's findings can be significantly affected by the particular analytical framework one adopts in studying evangelicals. Whether one chooses to view evangelicals in this country as a socio-religious group or as a religious movement, for example, significantly affects one's assessments of both the numerical strength and the political characteristics of evangelicals.[3]

For the purposes of this study, evangelicals will be viewed as a socio-religious group. Evangelicals are defined as those Protestants who emphasize that conversion is the first step in the Christian life (that is, that salvation is obtained through confession of faith in Jesus Christ) and who regard the Bible as the basis of religious authority.[4] To identify evangelicals within the various surveys, therefore, three general operational measures are used: questions relating to the respondent's religious or denominational affiliation, questions relating to the respondent's "born-again" status, and questions relating to the respondent's view of the Bible.[5] Finally, because evangelicals are viewed as a socio-religious group, analysis is generally restricted to white respondents only.[6]

Political vs. Statistical Significance

What should constitute the criteria by which we determine whether or not a particular data pattern is important? Analysts frequently use a model of evaluation based upon random chance. If a statistical result occurs that is likely to happen only once in a hundred times, it is stated that the result is statistically significant at the .01 level. If it is likely to occur only once in a thousand times, it is stated that it is statistically significant at the .001 level. Some things that may be statistically significant, however, may not be politically significant. Though there may be a statistically significant increase in the number of left-handed voters within American society over time, such an increase is unlikely to be politically significant.

By contrast, something that does not have statistical significance can have political significance. Increments of change over two points of time may not be statistically significant but may be very significant politically. For example, assume that a typical survey accurately reflected the population being sampled and that the respondents accurately reported their votes cast for a particular office at one time and then again at another. Assume, too, that the reported votes cast for the Democratic candidate by these respondents changed only 2 per cent over the two points in time. Such a minimal change in the voting behavior of these respondents within surveys of conventional size (i.e., 1,200–2,000 respondents) would probably not attain statistical significance, but it would certainly be politically significant if the percentage of votes cast for the Democratic candidate had risen from 49 to 51 per cent of the vote.

This difference between statistical and political significance becomes important when one examines patterns of evangelical political attitudes and behavior over time. It may be, for example, that there has been a small but consistent increase in the percentage of evangelicals voting in recent presidential elections. Such a small increase may be statistically insignificant. But is it politically significant? This question, which is an important one for the task at hand, is hard to answer. Because there are margins of error associated with each survey, it is hard to determine whether such marginal changes across surveys are politically significant.[7] To a certain extent, the answer is in the eye of the beholder. What may appear to be politically significant to some readers may seem politically insignificant to others. Thus, interpretations of what the data suggest are all that can be offered. Without additional, more complete data (which frequently do not exist), it may be impossible to answer such questions with great confidence.

Data and Methods

A relatively large number of surveys are used here to track what changes, if any, have been evident among evangelicals over the course of the 1976, 1980, 1984, and 1988 presidential elections. Because certain surveys have used somewhat different wording for those questions tapping evangelical respondents (and because we know that different wording yields somewhat different results), the surveys are grouped into three different categories: (1) Gallup, *Los Angeles Times*, and National Opinion Research Center (NORC) surveys, (2) the National Election Studies conducted by the Center for Political Studies (CPS) at the University of Michigan, and (3) the 1988 National Election Day Exit Poll Survey conducted by CBS News and the *New York Times*.

Within the first category are seven different surveys that were conducted by different organizations over time but that used identical questions in tapping evangelical respondents.[8] To be classified as an evangelical within the first category of surveys, a respondent had to be a Protestant who responded affirmatively to the question "would you say that you have been 'born again' or have had a 'born-again' experience—that is, a turning point in your life when you committed yourself to Christ"; who stated either that the Bible is the actual word of God and is to be taken literally, word for word, or that the Bible is the inspired word of God; *and* who reported having tried to encourage someone to believe in Jesus Christ.[9]

Within the second category are the three University of Michigan surveys conducted during the course of presidential elections in 1980, 1984, and 1988. To be classified as an evangelical within these surveys, a respondent had to be a Protestant who responded affirmatively to the question of whether or not he or she had a "deep religious experience which [had] transformed their lives," and who expressed the view that "the Bible is God's word and all it says is true."[10]

The 1988 National Election Day Exit Poll Survey conducted by CBS News and the *New York Times* constitutes the third category. This particular survey is different from the others in several ways. First, it identified evangelicals by employing a single self-identification question that asked each respondent to indicate whether he or she was a "Fundamentalist or Evangelical Christian." While this measurement approach has certain advantages and certain disadvantages,[11] it has not been widely employed in national surveys until recent years and cannot be used, therefore, to track changes within the evangelical community before the late 1980s.[12] This survey is limited, moreover, to those who actually cast ballots on election day. Thus, while it may be representative of voters who went to the polls in November 1988, it is not representative, as are the other surveys, of the American electorate generally, and it cannot answer certain types of questions (e.g., do evangelicals turn out to vote at rates higher than, comparable to, or lower than non-evangelicals?). This exit-poll survey does, however, have a major advantage in terms of its size: over 11,500 people responded. Its size permits comparisons of evangelicals and non-evangelicals among both white and black respondents. Consequently, this survey is employed when analysis shifts to the New Religious Right's potential to attract votes from within the black community.

Because different operational measures for tapping evangelicals were employed in different national surveys, changes over time are analyzed separately for each of the first two measurement approaches. Fortunately, however, the surveys for these two measurement approaches cover roughly the same span of time. Thus, while the exact percentages may vary by measurement approach, one can nevertheless assess whether the resultant patterns associated with one category of surveys are evident in the other category as well. If such patterns are present, one can then have greater confidence that even the small increments of change evident in the surveys reflect true, rather than simply random, change.

The Number of Evangelicals

Even when evangelicals are defined somewhat narrowly in terms of a socio-religious group, they constitute a sizable, and apparently growing, segment of the American electorate. Table 1 presents the relative distribution of white evangelicals within the American electorate since 1976. Because different operational measures for tapping evangelicals were employed in the two categories of surveys, change over time is presented in two separate columns. As can be seen from Table 1, different surveys and different operational measures tend to yield different results regarding the relative size of the evangelical voting bloc (with the Gallup/LA Times/NORC surveys yielding somewhat higher estimates than the Michigan surveys). It would appear that at the close of the past decade evangelicals constituted somewhere between one-fifth and one-quarter of the white electorate. As is true of any relatively large group of voters, the sheer number of evangelicals contributes to making them a group with potentially high political significance.

Moreover, the data suggest that, if anything, the relative number of evangelicals has grown slightly over the course of the past decade. While the Gallup/LA Times/NORC sequence of surveys (hereafter referred to simply as the Gallup surveys) reveals some variation in the percentage of evangelicals, the overall pattern suggests that there has been an increase over time. This interpretation is based on two facts: (1) the percentages of evangelicals toward the end of

TABLE 1

Percentage of Evangelicals Among White Americans

GALLUP/LA TIMES/NORC				CENTER FOR POLITICAL STUDIES			
Month	Year	Evan.	(Number)	Month	Year	Evan.	(Number)
Aug.	1976	21	(2,422)				
Aug.	1980	23	(2,442)	Nov.	1980	15	(1,222)
May	1983	20	(2,320)				
Nov.	1984	24	(2,161)	Nov.	1984	17	(1,708)
July	1986	25	(2,039)				
Aug.	1987	32	(1,159)				
March	1988	26	(1,234)	Nov.	1988	18	(1,698)

the decade are consistently greater than those evident before the mid-1980s, and (2) the Michigan data reflect the same pattern.

The Social Composition of Evangelicals

In terms of their social composition, evangelicals tend to differ from non-evangelicals in a variety of ways. The extent to which they differ depends, in part, on the way the groups are defined, and the particularities of individual surveys. Nevertheless, regardless of which particular category of surveys one analyzes, the patterns of social differences between white evangelicals and non-evangelicals are consistent.

Table 2 presents data about the social composition of white evangelicals and non-evangelicals over time. It is evident from the table that white evangelicals are more likely than white non-evangelicals to be female, Southern, somewhat older in age, and less likely to have attended college. In data not presented here, these surveys also reveal that evangelicals are more likely than non-evangelicals to live outside of major urban centers of American life, to be married, and to have children. Moreover, these latter differences in "lifestyle" are not simply a function of the age differences between evangelicals and non-evangelicals. As can be seen in the bottom part of Table 2, young evangelicals are consistently more likely to be married (and to have children—data not shown) than non-evangelicals their age.

Given that social characteristics of the electorate generally change slowly over time, one would not anticipate major changes in the social composition of evangelicals and non-evangelicals over the course of the relatively short period analyzed here. Nevertheless, there does appear to be one pattern of change evident in Table 2: the increased level of education found among both evangelicals and non-evangelicals. Yet, while both groups of surveys reveal a growth in the percentage of college-educated evangelicals since 1976, evangelicals continue to lag behind non-evangelicals. To a certain extent, however, educational differences between white evangelicals and non-evangelicals appear to be a function of age differences between the two groups. When one examines various data on the level of education among young evangelicals and young non-evangelicals

TABLE 2

Social Composition of White Evangelicals and Non-evangelicals

Social Characteristics	GALLUP/LA TIMES/NORC		CENTER FOR POLITICAL STUDIES	
	Non-evan.	Evan.	Non-evan.	Evan.
% *Female*				
1976	51	64	—	—
1980	51	64	54	67
1984	49	59	53	65
1988	54	61	53	66
% *Southern*				
1976	18	40	—	—
1980	18	42	24	48
1984	19	47	21	45
1988	—	—	23	55
% *Some College*				
1976	32	23	—	—
1980	33	22	42	32
1984	43	27	46	34
1988	45	36	46	37
% *Under 35 Years*				
1976	41	30	—	—
1980	40	27	39	36
1984	39	34	38	35
1988	34	28	33	29
% *Under 35 Years Who Are Married*				
1976	—	—	—	—
1980	—	—	57	67
1984	49	58	55	70
1988	39	73	50	60

(i.e., those under 35 years of age), one finds that such educational differences either disappear or are significantly diminished. Consequently, in terms of educational attainment, the gap between white evangelicals and non-evangelicals does seem to be narrowing.

Probably the most politically significant socio-demographic characteristic of white evangelicals is their relatively high concentrations in the South. Whereas evangelicals comprise slightly over one-tenth of the white electorate outside the South, they comprise close to one-third of the white electorate within the South.[13] This geographical concentration is likely to enhance their potential power over the course of the next several presidential elections. In recent years the South, providing a bloc of electoral college votes, has increased in national prominence and electoral importance. Given their concentration in Southern states, evangelicals may greatly affect the political direction of the South, and partisan attempts to capture Southern electoral college votes must take into account both the presence of evangelical voters and the changes taking place within their ranks.

The Politicization of Evangelicals

The relative size and social composition of a bloc of voters is of little importance politically if its members remove themselves from the political process. Prior to the 1980s, evangelicals were less likely than their non-evangelical counterparts to be politically involved.[14] But in the late 1970s and the early 1980s, considerable efforts were made to register evangelical voters and to insure that they turned out at the polls on election day. Many of these efforts were initiated by the New Religious Right and its most widely recognized component organization, the Moral Majority.[15] In fact, the New Religious Right, while composed of various religious groups, found its major base of support among fundamentalist evangelicals, a subgroup of evangelicals that had historically shied away from political life.[16]

Is there any evidence to suggest that these efforts have helped to increase the level of politicization among evangelicals? Are evangelicals today more likely to be registered to vote than they were in the mid-1970s? Has there been an increase in the percentage of evangelicals who, over the past several presidential elections, turned out to vote on election day? Tables 3 and 4 address these questions.

Table 3 presents the percentages of white evangelicals and non-evangelicals who reported that they were registered to vote or had voted in the previous presidential election within the Gallup surveys. The data suggest that evangelicals, as a whole, were already relatively politicized just before the 1976 presidential election. Unfortunately, because the particular measurement items used to identify evangelical respondents had not been employed in any national survey prior to this point, one cannot determine whether

TABLE 3

Politicization of White Evangelicals and Non-evangelicals:
Gallup/LA Times/NORC Data

	Aug. 1976	Aug. 1980	May 1983	Nov. 1984	July 1986	Aug. 1987	Mar. 1988
Evangelicals							
% registered	73	74	67	—	79	80	—
% voted in last							
pres. election	—	—	—	70	—	—	73
Non-evangelicals							
% registered	70	72	73	—	74	73	—
% voted in last							
pres. election	—	—	—	73	—	—	68

this level of politicization among evangelicals reflected a long-standing phenomenon or whether it was uniquely high in response to the Carter candidacy of that year. Regardless, the percentage of evangelicals who in August 1976 reported that they were registered to vote (73 per cent), slightly exceeded that of non-evangelicals (70 per cent). Similarly, at the advent of the general-election campaign in 1980, a slightly higher percentage of white evangelicals than non-evangelicals reported that they were registered to vote (74 per cent versus 72 per cent). Because these percentages among evangelicals prior to the election of Ronald Reagan are roughly equivalent, they can be used as a base line by which to evaluate whether, despite the relatively high level of politicization already evident among evangelicals, there has been any further increase in politicization within their ranks.

Given this base line, it would appear, first of all, that evangelical involvement in politics toward the end of Reagan's first administration declined somewhat, relative both to the earlier levels and to the level displayed by non-evangelicals. In May 1983 the percentage of evangelicals who reported that they were registered to vote was less than it had been in August 1980, while the corresponding percentage reported by non-evangelicals remained relatively stable over the same period. This lower level of politicization was further evident in the lower level of voter turnout reported by evangelicals than non-evangelicals following the Reagan-Mondale contest in November 1984 (70 per cent versus 73 per cent, respectively). On the other hand, Table 3 also suggests that evangelicals showed some increased politicization during the latter years of the Reagan administration. Both the July 1986 and the August 1987 surveys indicate a 6-percentage-point increase in registered voters among evangelicals over the levels evident prior to Reagan's election in 1980, and that this increase transpired while no corresponding increase in registration took place among non-evangelicals.

Many of these same patterns of change in politicization levels are evident when one examines levels of voter turnout. Table 4 employs CPS data and presents reported levels of voter turnout among white evangelicals and non-evangelicals over time. Since voter turnout tends to be lower in the South than outside the South, the table also presents the percentages of voter turnout among evangelicals and non-evangelicals when one controls for geographical location.

It would appear from Table 4 that the reported level of voter turnout among evangelicals and non-evangelicals alike has varied considerably since 1976. Nevertheless, these data suggest that evangelical voter turnout surged in 1980, the only year in which voter turnout among evangelicals exceeded that among non-evangelicals. This 1980 surge appears to have been a deviation from previous patterns in that evangelicals in 1980 also reported that they were less likely to have voted in all or most of the previous presidential elections than did non-evangelicals (data not shown).[17] Between 1980 and 1984, the percentage of evangelicals who reported voting declined, while it increased among non-evangelicals. This pattern of lower voter turnout among evangelicals in 1984 is

TABLE 4

Voter Turnout Among White Evangelicals and Non-evangelicals:
CPS Data

	1976*		1980		1984		1988	
	Non-evan.	Evan.	Non-evan.	Evan.	Non-evan.	Evan.	Non-evan.	Evan.
% All Respondents	65	62	72	77	76	70	72	71
% Non-South	67	66	73	75	78	75	75	80
% South	61	58	66	79	69	62	61	61

*The 1976 data are based upon the recall of the respondents in 1980.

consistent with the Gallup data shown in Table 3. Finally, the level of voter turnout among evangelicals stabilized between 1984 and 1988, while it declined somewhat for non-evangelicals. As a result, the level of voter turnout reported by evangelicals in 1988 was virtually equivalent to that reported by non-evangelicals (71 versus 72 per cent, respectively). Overall, therefore, the data presented in Table 4 suggest that politicization among evangelicals over the past fifteen years has increased. Whereas evangelicals were apparently less prone than non-evangelicals to be politically involved in an earlier era, they now appear to be just as politicized as non-evangelicals.

Much of this waxing and waning of evangelical voter turnout seems to be tied to changing levels of turnout among Southern evangelicals. As shown in the bottom portion of Table 4, there has been a pattern of increased turnout at the polls among evangelicals outside the South. And though Southern evangelicals appear to have surged to the polls in 1980, they seem to have lost some of their political fervor following that election. In both 1984 and 1988, the level of turnout reported by Southern evangelicals was nearly 20 percentage points lower than it had been in 1980. It would appear, then, that the surge in politicization evident among evangelicals in the late 1970s and early 1980s was due largely to the increased levels of politicization exhibited by Southern evangelicals. However, while there has been a surge and subsequent decline in voter turnout among Southern evangelicals, the level of politicization among evangelicals outside the South has shown a slow but sustained growth.

Partisanship Among Evangelicals

Given the lack of appropriate survey questions for identifying evangelicals, tracing changes in their partisan identifications over an extended period of time is difficult. Nevertheless, indirect evidence suggests that before the 1970s evangelicals were predominantly Democratic,[18] probably due, in part, to their heavy concentration in the historically Democratic Southern states.[19]

Tables 5 and 6 attempt to assess the level of change in partisanship among white evangelicals and non-evangelicals over the past fifteen years. Table 5 provides data taken from the Gallup surveys, while Table 6 presents related data taken from the CPS surveys. These tables reveal changes in the reported partisan self-identifications, expressed presidential voting preferences, and expressed congressional voting preferences of evangelicals and non-evangelicals over time.

As can be seen from Table 5, the Gallup data from August 1976 and August 1980 suggest that the percentage of Republicans among evangelicals was greater than that found among non-evangelicals. Yet, at the same time, the percentage of Democrats among evangelicals actually exceeded the percentage of Republicans, with 42 and 49 per cent of evangelicals classifying themselves as Democrats in 1976 and 1980, respectively (data not shown). Democrats outnumber Republicans among evangelicals in the 1980 CPS data as well (41 per cent classified themselves as Democrats, 33 per cent as Republicans).

Since 1980 a pronounced shift toward increased Republicanism has taken place in the partisan identifications and partisan voting among non-evangelicals. However, an even stronger pro-Republican shift has been evident among evangelicals. First, the percentage of self-classified Republicans among evangelicals and non-evangelicals appears to have increased during the years of Reagan's first

TABLE 5

Partisanship of White Evangelicals and Non-evangelicals:
Gallup/LA Times/NORC Data

	Aug. 1976	Aug. 1980	May 1983	Nov. 1984	July 1986	Aug. 1987	Mar. 1988
Evangelicals							
% Republican	34	34	35	45	25	21	40
% preferring/voting GOP pres. candidate	47	53	56	80	81	—	82
% preferring/voting GOP cong. candidate	48	42	—	65	51	—	—
Non-evangelicals							
% Republican	24	24	26	37	27	26	30
% preferring/voting GOP pres. candidate	41	48	54	63	74	—	66
% preferring/voting GOP cong. candidate	31	38	—	53	53	—	—

administration—regardless of whether the Gallup or CPS measures are used. This increase in Republican identifications did not transpire gradually over the course of Reagan's first term in office. Rather, the Gallup data suggest it occurred largely between May 1983 and November 1984, though other evidence indicates that it was already evident by September 1984.[20] Why this general increase in Republican identifications transpired within this relatively brief interval of time is not totally clear. Perhaps such gains were tied to the end of the recession or to the ongoing political debates associated with the presidential primaries and nominating conventions. Whatever the reason, a plurality of evangelicals classified themselves as Republicans when Reagan began his second term of office, whereas a plurality of evangelicals had classified themselves as Democrats prior to Reagan's election in 1980.

Whatever the gains in Republican partisan identifications that occurred during Reagan's first term, they did not continue during his second. The Gallup data suggest that such gains may well have dissipated during Reagan's second term, only to recover somewhat by March of 1988.[21] Nevertheless, the levels of GOP identification among evangelicals and non-evangelicals alike were lower in early 1988 than they had been in late 1984. But despite this decline in GOP identification among evangelicals between 1984 and 1988, a plurality of evangelicals still claimed Republican identifications in March of 1988. As a result, in early 1988, self-classified Republicans enjoyed a net partisan advantage of 11 percentage points over self-

TABLE 6

Partisanship of White Evangelicals and Non-evangelicals:
CPS Data

	1976*	1980	1984	1988
Evangelicals				
% Republican	—	33	37	38
% voting GOP pres. cand.	50	67	76	70
% voting GOP cong. cand.	—	57	55	58
Non-evangelicals				
% Republican	—	26	30	30
% voting GOP pres. cand.	53	62	61	56
% voting GOP cong. cand.	—	48	47	42

*The 1976 percentages are based upon the recall of the respondents in 1980.

classified Democrats among evangelicals, while among non-evangelicals self-classified Democrats enjoyed a net partisan advantage of 4 percentage points over Republicans (data not shown).

The data presented in Tables 5 and 6 both suggest that GOP gains in the electorate were halted during Reagan's second administration. At the same time, however, both tables underscore the strength of the GOP among evangelicals. At the end of 1988, self-classified Republicans enjoyed a net partisan advantage of 9 percentage points over self-classified Democrats among evangelicals, while among non-evangelicals self-classified Democrats enjoyed a net partisan advantage of 1 percentage point over Republicans (data not shown).

The same patterns of increased Republicanism are evident in the voting behavior of white evangelicals and non-evangelicals alike, though greater GOP gains appear to have been made among evangelicals than among non-evangelicals. The particular patterns of change seem to differ somewhat among evangelicals and non-evangelicals, and to vary somewhat according to data gathered by different survey organizations. In presidential races, the data in Tables 5 and 6 reveal an increased level of Republican preference and Republican voting since 1976. Though evangelicals did not support Bush in 1988 as widely as they supported Reagan in 1984, Bush still received more evangelical support in 1988 than Reagan did in 1980. The increased level of GOP identification among evangelicals is thus also associated with an increased level of GOP presidential voting.

With respect to voting for congressional candidates, the patterns are somewhat less clear. Though it is hard to demonstrate, the impact of incumbency in congressional voting may well account for this greater variation in voting patterns. Americans tend to express negative evaluations of Congress, yet they tend to vote for incumbent congressmen. If the partisan affiliation of the respondent's congressman were known, one could control for its effects and better assess the extent to which evangelicals have moved toward increased Republican voting for congressional candidates. Unfortunately, such information is not available with the surveys.

Despite the lack of such information, however, there are signs that the number of evangelicals voting for Republican congressional candidates may have increased to some degree in the 1980s. Both Tables 5 and 6 suggest that, at the very least, the level of evangelical voting for Republican congressional candidates has remained basically stable over time, while the Democratic control of the House of Representatives has simultaneously increased. As a result, evangelicals have been, and continue to be, more likely than non-evangelicals to vote for Republican congressional candidates.

Clearly, a variety of factors contribute to making a social group, any social group, politically important: its size, strategic location, distinctive political attitudes, level of political participation, and level of voting cohesion. On the bases of these criteria, evangelicals appear to have grown in political importance over recent presidential elections. Not only do evangelicals constitute a larger bloc of voters within the American electorate, but they predominantly reside in the South, a region of immense political importance because of its bloc of electoral-college votes and its growing number of congressional seats. Moreover, evangelicals continue in terms of various social- and foreign-policy issues, to express distinctive political attitudes, while they have increased both their level of political involvement and their level of voting cohesion. Judging by these five criteria, then, one can responsibly conclude that evangelicals have either maintained or increased their level of political importance since 1976.

Evangelicals and the New Religious Right

Although there has been a great deal of research conducted on both the New Religious Right and the evangelical Christian community, significantly less research has been conducted analyzing the nature of the relationship between the two groups.[22] All too frequently, analysts have treated the political activity of evangelicals and the political activity of the New Religious Right as if they were identical. Not all members of the New Religious Right are evangelical Christians, however, and not all evangelical Christians are members of the New Religious Right. The relationship between the two groups, which is likely to wax and wane over time, raises many questions.

Fortunately, the 1980, 1984, and 1988 CPS National Election

Studies contain items that help scholars identify both evangelical Christians and supporters of the New Religious Right. In addition to the previously discussed measures identifying evangelical respondents, these CPS surveys contained items that asked respondents to rate various social and political groups according to the negative or positive feelings they evoked. Respondents were asked to use a thermometer scale ranging from 0 degrees (extremely cold, negative feelings) to 100 degrees (extremely warm, positive feelings) to score the groups. "Evangelical groups active in politics, such as the Moral Majority," was one of the groups listed.[23]

Of course, this item indicates support for particular organizations rather than for the policies advanced by those organizations. Popular support for the Moral Majority has never been particularly high,[24] however, and support for the policies associated with the New Religious Right has always *exceeded* the level of support for the organizations tied to the New Religious Right.[25] Thus, the subsequent analysis, which focuses on "evangelical groups active in politics, such as the Moral Majority," is likely to underestimate the extent to which the mass electorate supports the issue positions of the New Religious Right.

Table 7 presents the average (i.e., mean) thermometer score given to the item "evangelical groups . . ." within different categories of respondents over time. The top part of Table 7 presents the mean scores as given by evangelical and non-evangelical respondents over the three presidential elections of the 1980s. Not too surprisingly, evangelicals were more likely than non-evangelicals to rate the "evangelical groups active in politics, such as the Moral Majority" item positively. More important, however, are several other patterns. First, non-evangelicals as a whole consistently rated groups such as the Moral Majority in negative terms. In fact, in 1980, when some thirty-four groups and institutions were included in the list, the Moral Majority ranked third from the bottom; only radical students and black militants received lower overall scores.[26] Similarly, in 1984 only black militants and gay men and lesbians ranked lower than the Moral Majority of the twenty-four groups used.[27] Second, a substantial drop in the favorable evaluation of "evangelical groups active in politics" occurred between 1984 and 1988. This was true among both evangelicals and non-evangelicals. In

TABLE 7

**Evaluation of "Evangelical Groups Active in Politics"
by White Respondents: CPS Data**

	MEAN THERMOMETER SCORES		
	1980	1984	1988
All Respondents			
evangelicals	59.9	60.2	52.9
(number)	(154)	(267)	(286)
non-evangelicals	44.0	41.4	33.8
(number)	(917)	(1,267)	(1,089)
Evangelicals Only			
evangelical Democrats	56.7	54.1	50.3
(number)	(58)	(85)	(81)
evangelical independents	59.7	60.1	51.2
(number)	(48)	(81)	(95)
evangelical Republicans	63.2	65.6	56.3
(number)	(47)	(97)	(109)
Republicans Only			
evangelical Republicans	63.2	65.6	56.3
(number)	(47)	(97)	(109)
non-evangelical Republicans	45.5	44.9	34.4
(number)	(249)	(408)	(330)

fact, by 1988 evangelicals themselves gave "evangelical groups active in politics" a mean thermometer score of only 52.9, a barely positive rating.

The middle portion of Table 7 examines the thermometer ratings given by evangelical respondents while controlling for their reported partisan identifications. All three partisan groups of evangelicals rated the Moral Majority positively, with evangelical Republicans expressing the highest level of affection for the Moral Majority and evangelical Democrats the lowest. More surprisingly, this portion of Table 7 reveals that the greatest slippage in evangelical support for "evangelical groups active in politics" occurred among those evangelicals who were self-classified independents and Republicans. Just what caused such slippage, particularly within the ranks of evangelical Republicans, is hard to say.[28] It may be that some of the rancor between the Bush and Robertson forces early in the 1988 campaign contributed to the decline of positive evaluations among evangelical Republicans.

The bottom portion of Table 7 examines the mean scores given to "evangelical groups active in politics" among evangelical and non-evangelical Republicans. Despite the growing role of evangelicals in the coalition of Republican voters, non-evangelical Republicans have consistently expressed negative evaluations of "evangelical groups . . . ." While the Republican party may say it desires to be a "big tent," some groups may be more welcome than others. A certain number of "country-club" Republicans are no doubt unhappy about the presence of Religious Right Republicans within the ranks of their party organization.[29]

In order to look at these evaluations from a different perspective, the scores given to the "evangelical groups . . ." item were classified into three categories: (1) negative, in which a respondent reported a score of 0–49 degrees; (2) neutral, in which a respondent reported a score of 50 degrees; and (3) positive, in which a respondent reported a score of 51–100 degrees. Table 8 presents the percentage of respondents giving positive, neutral, and negative ratings of the Moral Majority in 1980, 1984, and 1988. The table also presents the relative percentage of evangelicals found within each rating category over time. If one assumes that respondents who gave positive evaluations of the "evangelical groups . . ." item are supporters of the New Religious Right, it is possible to assess the extent to which evangelicals comprise the bloc of voters that might be labeled the "New Religious Right."[30]

As can be seen from the table, only 30 per cent of the white respondents in 1980 gave positive evaluations of the Moral Majority, whereas 43 per cent expressed negative evaluations. This distribution is what one might have expected given the mean scores reported in Table 7. Moreover, Table 8 shows that the percentage of respondents who expressed positive evaluations of "evangelical groups active in politics" monotonically declined between 1980 and 1988. By 1988 less than 20 per cent of the white respondents expressed positive evaluations, while a majority expressed negative evaluations.

Table 8 also reveals the percentage of evangelicals among those respondents who expressed positive feelings for "evangelical groups . . . such as the Moral Majority." It is evident from these data that evangelicals have constituted only a fraction of those respondents

TABLE 8

Evangelicals and Participation in the New Religious Right:
CPS Data

	THERMOMETER SCORES "Evangelical Groups Active in Politics"		
	Negative	Neutral	Positive
1980	43%	27%	30%
Non-evangelical	92%	89%	73%
Evangelical	8%	11%	27%
(Number)	(459)	(291)	(321)
1984	38%	23%	28%
Non-evangelical	92%	83%	69%
Evangelical	8%	17%	31%
(Number)	(647)	(399)	(488)
1988	56%	26%	18%
Non-evangelical	89%	75%	53%
Evangelical	11%	25%	47%
(Number)	(770)	(354)	(251)

who have supported the New Religious Right. In fact, in 1980, only slightly more than one-quarter of the supporters of the New Religious Right were evangelicals.[31] However, as evaluations of "evangelical groups . . ." have declined, the percentage of evangelicals among such supporters has increased. Consequently, by 1988 evangelicals comprised about one-half of the 18 per cent of the electorate who reported positive evaluations for the "evangelical groups . . ." item. Today, then, evangelicals constitute a large component, but less than a majority, of those who support the New Religious Right.

Support for the Religious Right

Why has the New Religious Right not been more successful in mobilizing support for its organizations? Several different explanations have been offered.[32] Some have contended that the New Religious Right might well be a victim, in part, of its own successes. Not only may it have been difficult for the New Religious Right to convey a sense of "crisis" to mobilize its supporters during the Reagan administration,[33] but the Reagan administration itself apparently coopted several New Religious Right groups—though it never really gave high priority to the enactment of their agenda.[34] Moreover, as suggested above, organizations such as the Moral Majority have not drawn nearly the level of support from their potential bases as might be expected. While evangelicals, as a whole, have been positively inclined toward "evangelical groups active in politics," their evaluations of such groups have been far from overwhelmingly positive. In fact, many evangelicals have expressed either neutral or negative evaluations of such groups.

What, then, differentiates those respondents who support "evangelical groups active in politics" from those evangelicals who do not express positive evaluations for such groups? In order to analyze the various social and political differences among them, respondents were separated into three categories: (1) supporters of the New Religious Right, i.e., those expressing positive scores on the Moral Majority item; (2) the target constituency, i.e., those evangelical Christians not reporting positive scores for the Moral Majority item; and (3) others.[35]

If the organizations of the New Religious Right wish to expand its support within the target constituency of white evangelicals, they need to know the social and political characteristics of this constituency and how its members differ from present supporters of the New Religious Right. The data presented in Table 9 reveal various social and political differences between supporters of the New Religious Right and its target constituency, and how they vary over time.

Socially, those characteristics that tend to differentiate supporters of the New Religious Right from its target constituency changed little over time. Members of the target constituency, that is, evangelicals who failed to express positive support for "evangelical groups active in politics," were more likely than supporters to be younger, female, Southern, and without any college education. Such social characteristics have also been historically associated with a lower level of voter turnout.

In fact, this target constituency does appear to be somewhat less likely to vote on election day, and somewhat more likely to be Democratic in partisan identifications, than are respondents who fall within the other two categories. Nevertheless, despite the

TABLE 9

Social and Political Characteristics of New Religious Right Constituencies: CPS Data

CONSTITUENCIES OF THE NEW RELIGIOUS RIGHT

(Number)	SUPPORTERS			TARGET			OTHERS		
	1980 (321)	1984 (488)	1988 (251)	1980 (98)	1984 (142)	1988 (195)	1980 (803)	1984 (1,089)	1988 (1,252)
% of population	26	28	15	8	8	12	66	63	74
% female	61	59	59	68	69	68	53	52	53
% Southern	28	31	32	51	50	50	24	19	32
% some college	37	39	45	29	26	28	43	49	46
% 18–34 yrs.	38	35	27	31	36	31	39	38	33
% 56+ yrs.	32	28	29	40	39	39	29	28	30
% high church attend.	40	37	48	38	39	40	21	20	21
% Democrats	31	27	28	44	40	31	37	36	31
% Republicans	32	38	38	31	27	33	24	29	30
% voted	71	75	76	74	66	67	73	76	72
% GOP pres. cand.	73	75	69	61	71	66	59	57	55
% GOP cong. cand.	63	54	57	54	56	50	44	45	41

greater Democratic proclivity, members of this target constituency are still fairly Republican in their voting patterns. This latter pattern suggests, albeit indirectly, that there may still be some potential for New Religious Right organizations to expand their support within the ranks of this target constituency. Obviously, expanding its base of support would enhance the New Religious Right's potential to serve as a significant force in American electoral politics.

However, certain factors may limit this expansion. First of all, some groups within this target constituency may be riper for mobilization than others.[36] Social and economic conservatives among white evangelicals are the groups more likely to be mobilized, while liberals and racial conservatives within the ranks of evangelicals are less likely.[37] Second, though the New Religious Right has been relatively successful in building a coalition across theological streams that have, at times, been somewhat antagonistic toward one another,[38] there is evidence that those identifying with specific theological traditions—fundamentalists and charismatics, for example—tend to support different figures or organizations of the New Religious Right.[39] Thus, any efforts on the part of the New Religious Right to mobilize further the evangelical community must also contend with the theological divisions evident within American evangelicalism—divisions that may dampen potential support for the policies and candidates advanced by the New Religious Right.

Blacks and the New Religious Right

One potential source of increased mobilization that political strategists have suggested lies within the black community.[40] The notion that there are few conservatives among black voters is widespread but wrong; a substantial percentage of blacks classify themselves as political conservatives.[41] Moreover, a higher percentage of evangelicals are found among blacks than whites.[42] Given this presence of evangelicals and political conservatives within the black community, a potential base of support for the New Religious Right may well exist among blacks.

To better assess this possibility, data were analyzed from the CBS/ *New York Times* National Election Day Exit Poll Survey of 1988. As mentioned earlier, this data source has the advantage of containing a very large number of randomly selected voters (11,645), which enables one to identify a large enough number of black evangelicals to make meaningful comparisons between evangelicals and non-evangelicals among both white and black voters.

Table 10 presents selected social and political characteristics of white and black voters in the 1988 election. The political characteristics of black voters suggest that possible attempts on the part of the New Religious Right to mobilize black voters do hold some promise but also present some distinct problems. While nearly twice as many black voters as white voters classified themselves as political liberals, for example, over two-thirds of them did not do so. In fact, blacks were much more likely to label themselves as moderates than liberals, and over 20 per cent of the black voters classified themselves as political conservatives. This distribution of ideological orientations among black voters in 1988 should offer some encouragement to the New Religious Right.

Though less than one-third of the black voters classified themselves as political liberals, however, nearly 80 per cent labeled themselves as Democrats. This latter characteristic of blacks is important, as voters are much more likely to vote on the basis of their partisan identifications than their ideological orientations. Thus, whenever the New Religious Right chooses to throw its

TABLE 10

Comparison of White and Black Voters:
CBS/*New York Times* Exit Poll of 1988

(Number)	WHITES (9,475)	BLACKS (1,494)
Social Characteristics		
% under 45 years	57	66
% males	47	45
% Southern	25	36
% college graduates	36	25
% family income $50,000 +	25	14
Political Characteristics		
% liberal	17	31
% conservative	35	22
% Democrat	34	79
% Republican	37	7

support to Republican candidates (as it most often does), it confronts some very serious obstacles to attracting black support, given the overwhelmingly Democratic inclinations found among black voters.

Black Conservatives

Nevertheless, more than 20 per cent of the black voters classified themselves as political conservatives. One out of every five black voters could be, therefore, a potential supporter of the New Religious Right. Black conservatives, however, are not necessarily similar to white conservatives in terms of their political attitudes and behaviors. Labeling themselves political conservatives may reflect either a relative assessment of, or an adherence to, some particular political philosophy. What it means to be a political conservative among black voters may be different from what it means among white voters. To what extent, then, are white and black conservatives alike? Is there any evidence to suggest that black conservative voters might be mobilized to support the policies and candidates advanced by the New Religious Right?

Table 11 examines various social characteristics, issue priorities, and political behaviors reported by white and black conservatives and non-conservatives. As the first part of Table 11 shows, white and black conservatives tend to share certain social characteristics. For example, males make up a higher percentage of conservatives than non-conservatives among both white and black voters. Likewise, Southerners are more likely to be found within the ranks of conservatives than non-conservatives, regardless of race. On the other hand, in terms of age, education, and family income, conservative and non-conservative blacks were more alike than were white and black conservatives. Moreover, the relationship between being an evangelical and being a political conservative seems to be different among white and black voters. Among white voters, evangelicals were nearly three times more likely to be found within the ranks of political conservatives than outside, but among black voters, evangelicals were just as likely, if not more likely, to be found outside their ranks.[43]

The second part of Table 11 presents the issue priorities expressed

TABLE 11

**Comparison of White and Black Self-classified Political Conservatives:
CBS/New York Times Exit Poll of 1988**

	WHITES		BLACKS	
	Non-cons.	Cons.	Non-cons.	Cons.
(Number)	(6,366)	(3,109)	(1,200)	(294)
Social Characteristics				
% under 45 years	58	56	66	69
% males	45	52	43	50
% Southern	22	30	34	43
% college graduates	35	37	25	24
% family income $50,000 +	24	26	14	15
% evangelical	6	18	8	7
Issue Priorities				
% punishing criminals	15	25	19	23
% helping middle class	29	16	34	30
% environment/pollution	14	7	7	6
% econ. prosperity/jobs	23	25	32	30
% federal deficit	14	10	8	9
% not raising taxes	12	17	14	20
% defense spending	7	10	5	4
% US-USSR relations	6	8	1	5
% abortion	6	10	3	4
Political Behavior				
% voted Reagan in 1984	59	92	14	31
% voted Bush in 1988	44	84	7	19
% voted GOP Cong. cand.	39	68	10	19
% voted GOP Sen. cand.	38	71	12	19
% always vote Democratic	27	9	81	76

by conservative and non-conservative respondents among both white and black voters. Respondents were asked to identify which one or two of the nine issues listed they believed were most important in the 1988 election. The figures reflect the percentage of respondents who checked a particular issue as one of their two most important in the campaign. Given the "forced choice" associated with these nine issues, it is not surprising that there is considerable similarity, regardless of ideological orientations, in the issue salience for white and black voters. Those issues having the highest percentages among white conservatives—namely, punishing criminals, helping the middle class, economic prosperity and jobs, and not raising taxes—were virtually the same as those having the highest percentages among the remaining three categories of voters. The issues that were identified as the most important in the campaign of 1988 did not seem to vary by the ideological or racial characteristics of the respondents.[44]

Nevertheless, some issues were more salient for conservative than non-conservative voters among both white and black respondents. For example, conservatives were more likely than non-conservatives, regardless of race, to cite punishing criminals and not raising taxes as important, and were somewhat less likely than non-conservatives to cite helping the middle class as important. These similarities suggest that with regard to certain issues, political conservatism means much the same thing among white and black voters, and that when the banner of political conservatism is waved on these issues, both white and black conservatives may well be mobilized to act in concert.

On the other hand, some issues tied to political conservatism among white voters do not appear to be so among black voters. For example, the issue of abortion was more salient for white than for black voters, and white conservatives were almost twice as likely to cite it as a major issue than were white non-conservatives. But the percentage of black conservatives citing the issue of abortion ranked lowest, and was virtually identical to the percentage of black non-conservatives citing the issue. Thus, the issues that mobilize white conservative voters may not be the ones that would mobilize black conservative voters. One cannot simply assume that the political conservatism of black voters is similar to the political conservatism of white voters. Any attempt on the part of the New Religious Right to mobilize black conservatives will, therefore, need to take into account how political conservatism is understood within the black community, and the ways in which it is similar to and different from conservatism outside that community.

Finally, Table 11 presents recent reported voting behavior of white and black conservatives and non-conservatives. While conservative blacks are indeed more likely to vote Republican than non-conservative blacks, their voting behavior differs markedly from that of conservative whites. While more than 90 per cent of the conservative whites reported voting for Reagan in 1984, for example, less than 33 per cent of the conservative blacks reported doing so. Conservative blacks vote overwhelmingly Democratic: less than 20 per cent of the conservative blacks reported voting for Bush, for a Republican congressional candidate, or for a Republican senatorial candidate in 1988. In fact, more that 75 per cent of the conservative blacks reported that they always vote Democratic. Given such Democratic partisanship in the voting patterns of conservative blacks, any attempt on the part of the New Religious Right to attract their votes for a Republican candidate will face serious obstacles.

Black Evangelicals

Would black evangelicals be a more sympathetic base than black conservatives for possible mobilization by the New Religious Right? An analysis of the CBS/*New York Times* exit-poll data provides a somewhat mixed answer. As can be seen in Table 12 below, white evangelicals reported ideological orientations and partisan identifications different from those of white non-evangelicals, but black evangelicals differed little from black non-evangelicals in ideological orientation and partisan identification. Approximately the same percentage of black evangelicals as non-evangelicals labeled themselves as political liberals (30 per cent), and approximately the

TABLE 12

Political Behavior of White and Black Evangelicals and Non-evangelicals: CBS/*New York Times* Exit Poll of 1988

	WHITES		BLACKS	
(Number)	Non-evan. (8,446)	Evan. (908)	Non-evan. (1,343)	Evan. (113)
Political Characteristics				
% liberal	19	8	31	30
% conservative	32	60	23	21
% Democrat	36	21	79	74
% Republican	35	52	7	10
Political Behavior				
% voted Reagan in 1984	68	88	17	25
% voted Bush in 1988	55	82	8	19
% voted GOP Cong. cand.	47	66	11	16
% vote GOP Sen. cand.	46	73	13	10
% always vote Democratic	22	9	81	62

same percentage of black evangelicals as black non-evangelicals classified themselves as Democrats (79 per cent and 74 per cent, respectively).

However, somewhat greater differences between black evangelicals and black non-evangelicals are evident when their reported voting behavior is examined. The percentage of black evangelicals who stated that they had voted for Reagan in 1984, for example, exceeded the percentage of black non-evangelicals. Likewise, more than twice as many black evangelicals than non-evangelicals reported voting for Bush in 1988 (19 per cent versus 8 per cent, respectively). And, finally, whereas 81 per cent of black non-evangelicals reported that they always voted Democratic, only 62 per cent of black evangelicals reported that they did so. Thus, while black evangelicals may mirror black non-evangelicals in terms of political disposition (i.e., in terms of ideological orientation and partisan identification), they do differ meaningfully in terms of voting behavior. Black evangelicals are much more Republican in their voting behavior than black non-evangelicals.

Thus, even among black voters, political conservatism and evangelicalism are both associated with a greater willingness to vote for Republican candidates. But, are these two factors interrelated? Does it make any difference in terms of voting Republican whether black conservatives are also evangelicals? Are black evangelical conservatives more likely to vote Republican than black non-evangelical conservatives?

Table 13 analyzes the voting behavior of evangelical and non-evangelical conservatives in 1988 among both white and black

TABLE 13

Political Behavior of Conservative Evangelicals and Non-evangelicals Controlling for Race: CBS/New York Times Exit Poll of 1988

	CONSERV. WHITES		CONSERV. BLACKS	
(Number)	Non-evan. (2,501)	Evan. (608)	Non-evan. (266)	Evan. (28)
% voted Reagan in 1984	91	97	29	58
% voted Bush in 1988	82	95	17	56
% voted GOP Cong. cand.	66	78	19	24
% voted GOP Sen. cand.	67	86	18	25
% always vote Democratic	10	6	78	39

voters. As the table indicates, even among political conservatives, whether or not one is an evangelical affects the likelihood of voting Republican. First, among white conservatives, evangelicals are somewhat more likely to vote Republican than non-evangelicals. For example, whereas 91 per cent of white non-evangelical conservatives reported voting for Reagan in 1984, almost every white evangelical conservative reported doing so (97 per cent). Likewise, while 82 per cent of the white non-evangelical conservatives voted for Bush in 1988, 95 per cent of white evangelical conservatives did so. Similar patterns are reflected in voting for congressional and senatorial candidates. The patterns are consistent across all five measures of voting behavior: white evangelical conservatives are more likely than non-evangelical conservatives to vote Republican.

The same pattern is apparent among black voters. While it was shown earlier in Table 11 that black conservatives, as a whole, did not vote very strongly for Republican candidates, they did give Reagan, in 1984, 31 per cent of their votes, which was quite a high percentage among blacks. Table 13, however, reveals that black evangelical conservatives reported substantially higher levels of voting for Republican candidates than black non-evangelical conservatives. Twice the percentage of black evangelical conservatives as non-evangelical conservatives reported voting for Reagan in 1984. An even greater difference in voting behavior was evident in 1988, when 56 per cent of black evangelical conservatives reported voting for Bush but only 17 per cent of black non-evangelical conservatives did so. While less than a majority of black evangelical conservatives reported voting for Republican congressional and senatorial candidates in 1988, such percentages were still consistently greater than the percentages found among black non-evangelical conservatives. Finally, more than 75 per cent of black non-evangelical conservatives reported always voting Democratic, but less than 40 per cent of black evangelical conservatives stated that they did so. Thus, the patterns are once again consistent across all five measures of voting behavior: black evangelical conservatives are more likely than black non-evangelical conservatives to vote Republican.

In summary, the New Religious Right would appear to face both obstacles and opportunities in any effort to win support among the blacks conservative community. Certainly, the obstacles pose serious challenges. The content of political conservatism may be different for black conservatives from what it is for white conservatives, and the strong Democratic proclivities of black conservatives mitigate against mobilizing them to vote for any Republican candidates who the New Religious Right may support. On the other hand, some opportunities may exist among black evangelical conservatives. If one assumes that voting for the Republican candidate constitutes a vote for the more conservative candidate, black evangelical conservatives were the most likely of the black groups analyzed to have voted for conservative candidates. Given such patterns, the New Religious Right might best place its efforts in mobilizing support among black evangelicals, particularly black evangelical conservatives.

In Conclusion

What does the future hold for evangelicals as a bloc of voters within the American electoral system? In the near future evangelicals are likely to continue to be a force in national politics, particularly on the side of more conservative forces.[45] At the same time, however, the locus of much evangelical political activity today has shifted to the state and local arenas. Such political activities tend to be less visible to the American public and to those scholars who focus on national politics because they are less likely to capture media attention. Evangelical political activities at the state and local levels may seem less novel and less significant to the news media today.[46] Yet, while they may be less visible, they are nevertheless likely to be important in forming a cadre of evangelical political activists, developing political skills among those activists, expanding evangelical political activism beyond the mere act of voting, and constructing broader political coalitions to achieve electoral and legislative goals. All these factors suggest that evangelicals are likely to retain, if not increase, their political importance over time.

Moreover, white evangelicals are likely to play a very large role in the future of the New Religious Right. Today they constitute a major, if not the major, constituency base for the movement. Nevertheless, their relationship to the New Religious Right has been a fluid one. At the beginning of the 1980s, they constituted only a fraction of the base of support for New Religious Right organizational efforts. As public opinion shifted during the late 1980s toward a more negative evaluation of the organizational manifestations of the New Religious Right—though not necessarily toward the policies they advocated—white evangelicals as a whole also became more critical of evangelical groups such as the Moral Majority. Yet, even as support for the Moral Majority declined within the general electorate, by the end of the 1980s white evangelicals constituted the bulk of its supporters. Despite their general conservatism, however, white evangelicals are a diverse lot. While more may still be available for mobilization by the New Religious Right, its efforts to strengthen its base will have to move beyond seeking only their support.

One means by which the New Religious Right can expand its base is to attempt to build effective relationships with black evangelicals. To do so, however, the movement will have to give much greater thought to solving those problems that are of special concern to the black community.[47] Certain policies that tend to be advocated by the New Religious Right (e.g. welfare reform) may, in the short run, work against the perceived interests of black evangelicals. But there are many issues on which the moral concerns of the New Religious Right and black evangelicals are likely to overlap (e.g., drug addiction, deterioration of the black family). If white and black evangelicals are able to join forces politically, the political significance of both evangelicals and the New Religious Right will be enhanced.

Yet other signs suggest that the political importance of evangelicals may wane. At least three different factors could produce such an outcome. The first of these relates to the changing demographic characteristics of evangelicals—particularly the increasing levels of educational attainment and geographical mobility evident within their ranks. These changes may well make it increasingly difficult for evangelicals to maintain their distinctive moral and social beliefs—beliefs that have helped to separate them from non-evangelicals and to forge evangelical identity. If evangelicals simply come to resemble those non-evangelicals who share similar sociodemographic characteristics, then their political importance as a distinct bloc of voters will disappear as well.

The second factor relates to changes in the political environment that confront evangelicals today. Historically, one major component of their political unity was their strong opposition to Communism generally and to the Soviet Union particularly. With the collapse of Soviet Communism, evangelicals have "lost" a major symbol/issue that served as a unifying agent in their issue positions. The loss of such a cementing issue could well affect their political cohesion. Perhaps the only present issue that might serve to replace Communism is that of abortion. However, while opposition to Communism tended to unite many evangelicals and non-evangelicals, the issue of abortion tends to divide them.

The third factor affecting the future of evangelical political involvement is the shifting theological emphasis and collective understanding evident in American evangelicalism today. In particular, the nature of the "enemy" in evangelical political involvement may once again be changing. Initially, many evangelicals believed that either "modernism" or "Communism" constituted the threat. During the decade and a half just past, the emphasis was placed on "secular humanism." Now, however, with growing attention being given to the "New Age Movement," some evangelicals have shifted their focus to the dark spiritual forces they believe are undergirding the present political struggle. It may not be too surprising, therefore, that some have moved to establish a new type of political activist—a prayer warrior complete with prayer "dog tags."[48] The widespread adoption of such a perspective among evangelicals, regardless of whether or not it is warranted, cannot fail to have important political ramifications. Not only is it likely that such an emphasis will lead to a more pessimistic view of politics and political activity, but, at a minimum, it is likely to divert evangelical energy from the immediate, direct, political activity that political leaders tend to heed.

Response

James L. Guth

NOBODY watches the political behavior of evangelicals more knowledgeably than Corwin Smidt. As this essay shows, he has grappled with and overcome the many limitations of national surveys for interpreting evangelical voting. Together with Lyman Kellstedt of Wheaton College, he has provided much of the really insightful work available to us. I am neither inclined nor equipped to quarrel with his interpretation of data. But I will try to put his comments in a wider religious and political context.

One key to the Religious Right's fate is whether the movement is tied primarily to evangelicalism, however defined, or has the potential to be a broad traditionalist alliance, uniting observant Christians and perhaps other faiths as well. Smidt's essay and others in this volume show that the early Christian Right groups neither mobilized the entire evangelical community nor evoked widespread support from others outside it. But this does not mean the movement has not permanently influenced our politics.

For several years I've been urging my evangelical colleagues, and others, to focus on what might be called "conservative Christianity," to see whether the evangelical resurgence may be what economists call "a leading indicator" of broader changes in American party politics.[1] I would argue that the evangelical "conversion" documented by Smidt is just one facet of a critical shift in religion's significance: we are moving away from the old ethno-cultural foundations of political parties toward something more like a European pattern, in which parties of the right draw disproportionately from the religiously observant, and parties of the left from more secular forces.[2] Such a cleavage would represent only one

James L. Guth is professor of political science at Furman University. His work on religion, politics, and the political activism of conservative Protestants has appeared in many scholarly journals and books.

dimension of future partisan alignments, but the harbingers of it are everywhere.

Religion and American Parties: The Ethno-Cultural Divide

Historically, of course, American political parties never sorted voters into religious and secular camps. The reason was quite simple: secularist parties held little appeal for Americans who were, and remain, among the most religious peoples in the developed world. Americans' atypical religiosity had many sources. The absence of a state church tied to a traditional regime gave the left no reason to promote anti-clerical or secularist ideologies. Religious voluntarism allowed entrepreneurs to shape institutions and beliefs to "market" demands: there was a religious product for everyone's taste—and if not, one would soon appear. And as Louis Hartz pointed out long ago, America has always been a "fragment" society, and our "fragments" were often religious ones that abandoned older locales to seek religious autonomy.[3] The hostility attending the juxtaposition of such groups, once they arrived, reinforced religious observance as a mark of communal solidarity.

In this environment, political secularism or anti-clericalism was impossible. Not that religion was politically irrelevant; to the contrary, as ethno-cultural historians remind us, religion was often the very core of our party system.[4] Although their jargon differs, all these scholars perceive a permanent battle between Republican-oriented Protestant pietists and evangelicals, with their reformist bent, and members of minority religious traditions—like Catholics, Jews, and others, often "liturgical" in outlook—who saw the Democratic party as a refuge from the meddling of moral reformers, the protector of ethnic customs, and the guardian of "personal liberty." Thus, Republicans and Democrats were equally religious but had competing visions of what faith meant for public life. And although New Deal class politics eventually obscured these old alignments, they retained a marvelous resilience even into mid-century.

Beginning in the 1970s, though, we began to sense a new religious dimension to American politics. To many it seemed that the conflicts characteristic of social and political modernization in

Europe were appearing here, as secular elites in social and political institutions battled the forces of "order and tradition" over the role of religion in public life, prayer in schools, control of educational institutions and curricula, sexual morality, and traditional social arrangements. Although the Moral Majority and its nemesis, secular humanism, were both caricatures, they represented real and emerging social divisions. As Robert Wuthnow, Wade Clark Roof, and William McKinney have argued so persuasively, the new American religious alignment has theological, moral, and social conservatives on one side, and religious and—increasingly—secular liberals on the other.[5]

The Political Consequences

How has this change influenced our party system? The answer is fairly direct: these two religious "clusters" show every sign of gravitating toward different parties. The GOP is rapidly becoming not only the party of business conservatism but of traditional social values as well. The Democrats now harbor secularists and religious liberals, as well as labor activists. Like the theological restructuring described by Wuthnow, Roof, and McKinney, partisan change is still in process and has not entirely replaced earlier ethnic and denominational configurations, but we can distinguish several precursors of realignment.

First, religious leaders themselves are more and more split between parties by fundamental theological beliefs. Since the 1960s, studies have shown that modernist clergy in mainline denominations have preferred the liberal party, the Democrats, while conservative ministers in those same churches favored the GOP. Now this pattern is appearing in traditionally Democratic constituencies —such as Southern Baptists, the Assemblies of God, the Churches of Christ, and many Pentecostal churches—where ministers are moving, almost *en masse*, toward the GOP, approving the party's conservative stance on social and moral issues such as prayer in school, abortion, tuition tax credits, gay rights, and sex education.[6]

Insofar as religious professionals convey political values to their people, the cues in orthodox churches are usually Republican. Pat Robertson's conversion and bid for the Republican presidential nomination is merely the tip of an enormous iceberg of clerical activism. A similar, though less pronounced, trend has appeared in the historically Democratic Catholic Church: unlike earlier appointees, bishops chosen by John Paul II are ecclesial, theological, and political conservatives—and Republicans.[7]

Of course, parishioners' politics may not reflect clerical influence. When asked how much political sway shepherds have over their flocks, the sheep usually reply "very little" or "none," while the shepherds claim "a lot." The truth is somewhere in between: fundamental religious and moral values taught from the pulpit or in other religious settings do ultimately shape political worldviews, if not the course of the next election.[8] In any case, we find religious professionals adopting "compatible" religious and political views. To find that a Southern Baptist pastor is a fundamentalist is tantamount to discovering that he (masculine pronoun chosen deliberately) is also a political conservative and Republican.

Just as clergy are adjusting party loyalties to fit their religious worldviews, so political activists are dividing along religious lines. Here the evidence is quite convincing, although it has received relatively little attention. Studies of party professionals, grass-roots activists, financial contributors, and various other political "junkies" all find sharp distinctions in the religious traits of Democratic and Republican party workers and leaders. Although the old ethno-cultural alliances persist on the surface, underneath alignments are shifting. By every measure, Republicans are more "religious" than Democrats: they belong to and attend church more often, regard religious values as more important, hold higher views of Scripture, have more orthodox beliefs, and generally conform to more traditional religious molds. Even in the South, arguably the most uniformly religious part of the country, there is now an enormous religious gap between Republican and Democratic white activists.[9]

Thus, the people who work party machinery, choose candidates, finance campaigns, and thereby set the political agenda, are increasingly distinguished by religious orientation. The parties' respective interest-group allies differ even more: the GOP's associated Christian Right, anti-feminist, and even small-business groups are, if anything, more religious than the party, while labor activists, feminists, environmentalists, and public-interest enthusiasts are even more secular than the Democrats.

Here, then, we have an emerging consensus among religious and political specialists. Have these new partisan divisions seeped down to the average voter? Political elites often fight pitched battles over issues barely even perceived by the electorate. Indeed, it was literally two generations after the New Deal before most voters caught on to economic-policy differences between the pro-business GOP and the pro-labor Democratic party. So it would not surprise us if voters exhibited only the slightest propensity to divide along these lines. Yet, in fact, they already have.

Although, as Smidt points out, poor data hamper our efforts to trace these developments over time, the evidence is mounting. As Smidt and others have shown, white Americans belonging to theologically conservative churches, claiming "born-again" experiences, and espousing orthodox beliefs are now voting Republican, and are beginning to identify more strongly with the GOP. Regular attenders in mainline Protestant churches are also much more Republican by vote and identification than less faithful co-parishioners. Even among black evangelicals there are, as Smidt and Clyde Wilcox have demonstrated, tantalizing hints of GOP inroads. Only among traditionalist Catholics has GOP growth faltered—at least according to some analysts.[10]

Not only do we have the thorough evidence that Smidt has presented, but other data as well. In the 1988 Southern Super Tuesday primaries, fully 20 per cent of all Republican primary voters were "born again," compared to only about 7 per cent of all whites voting in the Democratic primaries. And the Republican preference is more than just short-term liking for Ronald Reagan (or desire to vote for Pat Robertson): 1990 network exit polls showed traditionally religious voters choosing Republican congressional candidates as well.[11]

There is much to suggest, then, that the United States is developing a new religious component in its party system. Nevertheless, this trend may have limits and produce results quite unlike those in Europe. First, Americans are still too religious to permit parties to divide purely along religious-versus-secular lines. While the GOP will continue to target and attract religiously orthodox and morally traditionalist activists and voters, the Democrats will draw not only secular citizens but those holding modernist or less conventional religious views as well. Voters in some traditionalist churches may be slower to move to the appropriate camp than others. And the continued mixed nature of both party coalitions is likely to frustrate purists among both Christian Right Republicans and more secular Democrats.

The importance of these new party lines will also vary with the salience of issues: when the economy is weak, "pocketbook" politics will re-activate class-based New Deal party alignments. When international crises loom, religious cleavages may recede. But the flurry of religious controversy surrounding the Gulf crisis proves that even economic- and foreign-policy attitudes are shaped by religious worldviews. As the *Los Angeles Times Mirror* 1988 election studies showed, religious perspectives are often associated with seemingly unrelated policy perspectives. For example, "moralists" (what we have called "conservative Christians") are not just social-issue conservatives: they are protectionists on trade, favor a strong defense, think the country is still declining, see government programs as inefficient and wasteful, and praise Republican economic policies. "Seculars" are just as distinct on the other side.[12] Thus, these new religious constellations may well prove stronger, more pervasive, and probably more durable than many scholars think. If such is the case, Smidt has given us an early peek into the nature of party politics in the 1990s.

AFTERWORD

Half Full or Half Empty?

George Weigel

I N assessing the impact of the New Christian Right on American politics, much revolves around the question of what we mean by "success" and, in turn, what we mean by "politics."

By politics, do we mean simply the contest for power as measured by policy and regulations, legislators elected, residents of the White House, and membership on the federal bench? Or, in addition to all that, do we also mean what politics has meant in the West since the Greeks: namely, the continuing public debate about the good society, its norms and characteristics, and the ways in which we organize ourselves intellectually and morally to defend individual liberty and promote the common good?

On this latter, more venerable understanding of politics, I am inclined to be more optimistic about the accomplishments of conservative Christians in American public life during the 1980s than are several of the distinguished contributors to this volume. Some things have changed. And, measured by the admittedly softer criteria my more fluid conception of politics suggests, they have changed for the better.

The first thing that has changed was analyzed with great wisdom by Richard John Neuhaus in his seminal book *The Naked Public*

George Weigel, a Roman Catholic theologian, is the president of the Ethics and Public Policy Center. His most recent book is *The Final Revolution: The Resistance Church and the Collapse of Communism*.

Square. As Neuhaus persuasively argues, the New Christian Right "kicked a tripwire" in our national consciousness, alerting otherwise somnambulant people to the fact that the United States in the late 1970s was on the verge of all but establishing secularism as *the* legally protected form of philosophical and moral self-understanding in the American republic. The New Christian Right recognized this and challenged it—with the salutary result of reopening a national church-state (or better, religion-and-society) debate.

The New Christian Right was not the only factor in creating this new argument. Cardinal John O'Connor's and Representative Henry Hyde's interventions in the 1984 presidential-election debates played an important role. Nor is the debate resolved. The correlation of forces within the argument remains, to my way of thinking, unsatisfactory. There are disturbing signs that the Supreme Court, and now from its more conservative wing, is drawing the boundaries of "free exercise" far too narrowly. All that can be conceded.

And yet, having conceded that, I think we should still recognize, and with some satisfaction, that an argument is going on that wasn't going on before the New Christian Right entered the lists. Prior to the dramatic, and occasionally vociferous, entry of conservative Christians into the American public square, the unspoken assumption was that the gentle imposition of established secularism was simply the way things were in modernity, and particularly in that premier test case of modernity, the United States of America. *That* assumption, at least, has been routed, as even some in the intellectual and media elite admit, however grudgingly. Secularization has not triumphed; the United States is not Sweden, nor is it going to become Sweden. Having nailed that point down was, I think, a signal accomplishment of the New Christian Right—with, of course, a little help from its friends.

Some of the real-world implications of this shift in understanding are already evident. When People for the American Way, that quintessential antagonist of the New Christian Right and orthodox Catholics, is willing to concede, publicly, the mindlessness of public-school textbooks that fail to mention the religious origins of Thanksgiving or Martin Luther King, Jr.'s vocation as a Baptist minister, something of significance has happened. Before the emergence of the New Christian Right, questions like this about school materials were not even raised, at least in what passes for polite society. Now Norman Lear is raising them. I take that to be an important straw in the wind.

Nor should we minimize, in terms of this more elastic notion of politics, the accomplishments of the beleaguered right-to-life movement, in which conservative Protestants have played such a crucial leadership role. In its January 1973 story and editorial on the Supreme Court's decision in *Roe* v. *Wade*, the *New York Times* announced that the argument about abortion was over, finished, a done deal. But it wasn't. And the reason it wasn't was the right-to-life movement, whose success in keeping the issue alive in the 1980s was due in increasing measure to the work of evangelical and fundamentalist Christians. Thus when the Court reopened important dimensions of the abortion debate in its 1989 *Webster* decision, the *Times* and other mirrors of elite opinion had to admit that they had been wrong: the argument wasn't settled, and there were likely to be fifty arguments in the several states with which to contend in the future.

The New Christian Right and the broader right-to-life movement are, to be sure, frequently frustrated by the fact that they have not achieved their goal: maximum feasible legal protection for the unborn, rooted in a new societal and cultural consensus in which children are welcomed and cherished as a blessing. But even this frustration has to be measured against the remarkable tenacity of the movement that, in the face of a solid phalanx of opposition from virtually every other opinion-shaping and values-transmitting institution in our country, has not only survived but has begun to shift the terms of the public debate.

The New Christian Right also helped keep alive the question of parental choice in education during a decade in which even a conservative administration did little to break the public-school establishment's choke hold on the institutions, curricula, and philosophy of American elementary and secondary education. Christian day schools, under assault from the Justice Department and the Internal Revenue Service in the late 1970s, were, by the very fact of their existence a "sign of the times": a sign that the educational model the National Education Association (to take one key reference point) wished to establish as a monopoly was simply unacceptable to considerable numbers of Americans. Catholic schools and Jewish day schools were similar signs of contradiction, so to speak. But it was the political activism, in the narrower sense of politics, of conservative Christians that helped erect an important barrier against the pretensions of the monopolists. Though the issue of effective parental choice in education has not been satisfactorily resolved, of course, its continuing resonance tells us something notable about the success of the New Christian Right— again, with a little help from its friends.

Finally, we ought to recognize the important role that conservative Christians played in getting America out of the "malaise" in which it was supposed to have been stuck in the late 1970s. Perhaps it was never as bad as President Carter suggested; the 1980 election returns seemed to suggest that the candidate of malaise got trounced by the candidate of buoyant optimism about the American experiment. In any event, in the late 1970s there was a sense abroad in the land that the American moment may have passed and that the best that could be done was to negotiate a decent interval of retreat, after which other powers would come to the forefront of international affairs.

The New Christian Right never accepted the paradigm of the "racist, sexist, imperialist" America that underlay much of the cultural elite's disaffection with the American experiment. And by refusing to get on board this particular train of fashionable opinion, conservative Christians helped create the circumstances in which it was possible, again, to speak of the United States as a force for good in the world and as, for all its flaws and failures, a brave attempt to build a pluralistic democracy fit for human beings made in the image and likeness of God. No doubt some aspects of the New Christian Right's patriotism were distasteful, even excessive. But most conservative Christians knew, in their bones, that to pledge allegiance to a nation "under God" meant to affirm that America was not only a providential experiment in self-governance: it was also an experiment under judgment.

We cannot see the end of this process of national regeneration yet. It could still go wrong. But the fact that one can now talk, publicly, about a religious and moral affirmation of the American experiment in democratic pluralism is a good thing. And it is a good thing for which the New Christian Right can take a goodly measure of credit.

What the New Christian Right and its ecumenical and inter-religious allies did not do, of course, was move the debate from the level of "values" (a ubiquitous and slippery word in the national discourse) to the harder question of *norms*. Values can connote a moral egalitarianism in which we can each act according to our own principles, so long as nobody gets hurt. Functional libertarianism—which I take to be incompatible, over time, with the maintenance of a democratic republic—is the result.

But the new concern for values should not be dismissed out of hand. In however clumsy and unsatisfactory a fashion, it bespeaks an awareness of an irreducible moral dimension to American public life. It suggests, however inadequately, that there are questions of "ought" involved in the key questions of law, regulation, and policy. And so the next task for conservative Christians, and for all those who believe that morality is tied to an objective, normative order of things, is to figure out how to move the debate from values to norms. We have to rediscover how to say "you ought" to our fellow citizens again, rather than "I'd prefer." The New Christian Right cannot do this by itself; for one thing, it lacks a conception of morality that is capable of speaking across the pluralism of our society. But its intuitions, combined with the moral method of some of its ecumenical friends (I'm thinking in particular here of the Catholic reappropriation of the natural-law tradition as a "grammar" for the public debate), could help the country make some important progress on this front in the 1990s.

Is the glass half full or half empty? I incline, perhaps congenitally, to the view that it is half full. But however one measures the contents, there are a few important and just possibly decisive rays of sunshine coming through the glass.

Appendix

The conference upon which this book is based, "Evangelicals, Politics, and the New Religious Right: Assessing the Past, Scouting the Future," took place in Washington, D.C., November 14–15, 1990. The following persons participated:

Gary Amos, Regent University (Virginia)
Randall Balmer, Columbia University
Michael Cromartie, Ethics and Public Policy Center
Edward G. Dobson, Calvary Church,
    Grand Rapids, Michigan
Robert Dugan, National Association of Evangelicals
Terry Eastland, Ethics and Public Policy Center
Robert Booth Fowler, University of Wisconsin-Madison
James L. Guth, Furman University
Carl F. H. Henry, Prison Fellowship Ministries
James Davison Hunter, University of Virginia
Lyman A. Kellstedt, Wheaton College
Richard D. Land, Christian Life Commission,
    Southern Baptist Convention
George Marsden, Notre Dame University
Tom Minnery, Focus on the Family
Hubert Morken, Oral Roberts University
Kenneth Myers, *Stewardship Journal*
Richard Pierard, Indiana State University
Ralph Reed, Christian Coalition
A. James Reichley, Brookings Institution
James W. Skillen, Association for Public Justice
Corwin Smidt, Calvin College
Grant Wacker, Duke University

George Weigel, Ethics and Public Policy Center
Paul Weyrich, Free Congress Foundation
Donald Wildmon, American Family Association
Robert Wuthnow, Princeton University

Notes

Chapter 1

GEORGE MARSDEN

1. This point is suggested by John F. Wilson, "Religion, Government, and Power in the New American Nation," in *Religion and American Politics: From the Colonial Period to the 1980s*, ed. Mark A. Noll (New York: Oxford University Press, 1989), 77–91.

2. Daniel Walker Howe, *The Political Culture of the American Whigs* (Chicago: University of Chicago Press, 1979) provides an excellent discussion of these themes.

3. Robert Kelley, *The Cultural Pattern of American Politics* (New York: Knopf, 1979), 278–79.

4. Howe, *Political Culture*, 17, 18, 159, 167. A very detailed and sophisticated analysis of these patterns for a later period is offered by Philip R. VanderMeer, *The Hoosier Politician: Officeholding and Political Culture in Indiana: 1896–1920* (Urbana: University of Illinois Press, 1985), 96, 120.

5. Paul Kleppner, *Who Voted? The Dynamics of Electoral Turnout, 1870–1980* (New York: Praeger, 1982), 77–78. Cf. Kleppner, "From Ethnoreligious Conflict to 'Social Harmony': Coalition and Party Transformation in the 1980s," in *Emerging Coalitions in American Politics*, ed. Seymour Martin Lipset (San Francisco: Institute for Contemporary Studies, 1978), 41–59.

6. Kelley, *Cultural Pattern*, 285.

7. VanderMeer, *Hoosier Politician*, shows that in general the old patterns held in Indiana during the progressive era.

8. Quoted in James Hennesey, S.J., "Romanism, Catholics, and American Politics, 1900–1960: Altered Circumstances, Continuing Patterns," in *Religion and American Politics*, ed. Noll, 313.

9. Robert N. Bellah, "Civil Religion in America," *Daedalus* 96 (Winter 1967): 1–5.

10. Will Herberg, *Protestant-Catholic-Jew* (Garden City, N.Y.: Doubleday, 1955).

11. In *The New Shape of American Religion* (New York: Harper & Row, 1958), 76, 80, Marty was already talking about America's fourth faith as "secular humanism" (following John Courtney Murray in the usage). He also remarked that "it has an 'established church' in the field of public education." Presumably, discussions such as Murray's and Marty's were behind Justice Hugo Black's famous reference to "secular humanism" as a religion in a 1961 Supreme Court decision.

Such sober roots for the term run against claims (as in Sean Wilentz, "God and Man at Lynchburg," *The New Republic*, 25 April 1988, 36) of "the invention of secular humanism as a mass religion" by fundamentalists.

12. Grant Wacker's response, which was written in reaction to an earlier, less complete version of this paper, raises something like this issue.

13. Roman Catholics, of course, would add the interpretation of the Church. Liberal Protestants, civil-rights leaders, anti-war activists and others also appealed to God's law, though they have talked about it and interpreted it in ways differing from those of the Religious Right.

14. A number of observers have made this point. One of the most helpful is David C. Leege, "Coalitions, Cues, Strategic Politics, and the Staying Power of the Religious Right" (Paper delivered at the American Sociological Association, Washington, D.C., 11 August 1990). Leege, for instance, points out that fragmentation is especially likely among groups with strong sect-type traditions.

GRANT WACKER

1. Marsden elaborated and documented the interpretation he presents here in his popular college textbook *Religion in American Culture* (San Diego: Harcourt Brace, 1990).

2. Nancy Tatom Ammerman, *Baptist Battles: Social Change and Religious Confrontation in the Southern Baptist Convention* (New Brunswick, N.J.: Rutgers University Press, 1990), 73, 77.

3. I am indebted to Professor Howard G. Schneiderman of Lafayette College, Easton, Pennsylvania, for data on the Strong family, presented in a paper at the Society for the Scientific Study of Religion, Virginia Beach, Virginia, November 1990.

Chapter 2

ROBERT WUTHNOW

1. Robert C. Liebman and Robert Wuthnow, "Introduction," in *The New Christian Right: Mobilization and Legitimation*, ed. Robert C. Liebman and Robert Wuthnow (New York: Aldine, 1983), 1.

2. Although the phrase "New Christian Right" remains accurate as a label for the movement that emerged in the late 1970s, I shall refer mostly to the "Religious Right," partly because it is no longer "new" and partly because I want to suggest ways in which the broader movement may change in the years ahead. I am, therefore, not concerned with specific organizations (such as the Moral Majority or Christian Voice) but with the loosely organized movement consisting largely of conservative Christians (primarily Protestants) who are actively engaged in conservative politics.

3. The factors discussed here address the conditions I identified as having given rise to the Religious Right in my book, *The Restructuring of American*

Religion: Society and Faith Since World War II (Princeton: Princeton University Press, 1988), and more briefly in *The Struggle for America's Soul: Evangelicals, Liberals, and Secularism* (Grand Rapids, Mich.: Eerdmans, 1989), chapter 2. In those works I was attempting to account for the emergence of various conditions in American religion that came into prominence in the 1970s and 1980s, particularly the division between religious conservatives and religious liberals. Thus, my focus here is different, both in looking more toward the future, and in dealing specifically with the Religious Right. The conditions that contributed to polarization were not always the ones that nurtured the Religious Right. I am, therefore, interested in how well these broader conditions help us understand the present trajectory of the Religious Right.

4. The "this-worldly" orientation in American religion, I have argued, was not so much rooted in the kind of abstract theodicy that Weber identified but was framed within a discourse of "promise and peril" that became prominent in the United States after World War II and legitimated an exceptional level of religious activism; see Wuthnow, *Restructuring of American Religion,* 35–53.

5. Pre-millennialism is often included in the very definition of fundamentalism; see, for example, Nancy Tatom Ammerman, "North American Protestant Fundamentalism," in *Fundamentalism Observed,* ed. Martin Marty and R. Scott Appleby (Chicago: University of Chicago Press, 1990), chapter 1; for historical background on the emergence and varieties of American fundamentalism, see George M. Marsden, *Fundamentalism and American Culture* (Oxford: Oxford University Press, 1980).

6. For a broader discussion of the social conditions encouraging (or discouraging) millennial orientations, see Robert Wuthnow, *Meaning and Moral Order: Explorations in Cultural Analysis* (Berkeley: University of California Press, 1987), chapter 5.

7. Wuthnow, *Restructuring of American Religion,* 54–70.

8. For a brief statistical survey, see ibid., 17–29.

9. Some interesting comparative evidence to this effect is presented in John Boli, "Sweden: Is There a Viable Third Sector?" in *Between States and Markets: The Voluntary Sector in Comparative Perspective,* ed. Robert Wuthnow (Princeton: Princeton University Press, 1991), chapter 4.

10. George Gallup, Jr., *Religion in America, 1990* (Princeton: Princeton Religion Research Center, 1990), complete report.

11. Wuthnow, *Restructuring of American Religion,* 71–99; evidence on the weakening of denominational boundaries is also presented in Wade Clark Roof and William McKinney, *American Mainline Protestantism* (New Brunswick, N.J.: Rutgers University Press, 1987).

12. This cooperation should not be overemphasized, but see A. James Reichley, "Pietist Politics," in *The Fundamentalist Phenomenon,* ed. Norman J. Cohen (Grand Rapids, Mich.: Eerdmans, 1990), 98, for a similar argument.

13. On the Southern Baptist Convention, see Nancy Tatom Ammerman, *Baptist Battles: Social Change and Religious Conflict in the Southern Baptist Convention* (New Brunswick, N.J.: Rutgers University Press, 1990).

14. The concept of special-purpose groups and some evidence on their growing importance in American religion is developed in Wuthnow, *Restructuring of American Religion,* 100–31.

15. See Robert C. Liebman, "Mobilizing the Moral Majority," in *New Christian Right,* ed. Liebman and Wuthnow, 50–74, for the best discussion of these clergy networks.

16. Wuthnow, *Restructuring of American Religion*, 168–72.

17. Robert Wuthnow, *Acts of Compassion: Caring for Others and Helping Ourselves* (Princeton: Princeton University Press, 1991), chapter 5; this conclusion is drawn from discrimination and multiple-regression analyses of the factors distinguishing self-identified religious liberals from religious conservatives in a national survey I conducted in 1989 as part of a project on altruism and individualism in American culture; the question and analysis were identical to the ones I used earlier in examining the 1984 data.

18. On the importance of differences in social status, see John H. Simpson, "Moral Issues and Status Politics," in *New Christian Right*, ed. Liebman and Wuthnow, chapter 10.

19. On government growth and its consequences for religious participation, see Wuthnow, *Struggle for America's Soul*, chapter 5.

20. Simpson, "Moral Issues and Status Politics," in *New Christian Right*, ed. Liebman and Wuthnow, 186–205.

21. Wuthnow, *Acts of Compassion*, chapter 5.

22. A candid admission of this misconception is found in Kevin Phillips, "The Rise of the Religious Right," *New York Times*, 1 March 1988, A23.

23. Unpublished research done by James Davison Hunter at the University of Virginia suggests a relatively high level of anti-clericalism in the United States generally. It is, therefore, interesting to observe a "trend" of sorts in the national leadership of the Religious Right away from the parish clergy: from Jerry Falwell as a congregational pastor, to Pat Robertson as a pastor without a parish, to prominent laity such as Tim LaHaye, Beverly LaHaye, Charles Colson, and James Dobson.

24. Among the numerous studies of religious television, see especially Jeffrey K. Hadden, "Religious Broadcasting and the Mobilization of the New Christian Right," *Journal for the Scientific Study of Religion* 26 (1987): 1–24.

25. For more detail, see Wuthnow, *Struggle for America's Soul*, chapter 6.

26. For a supportive argument that fundamentalism does not constitute a threat to basic democratic ideals in American society, see Richard John Neuhaus, "Fundamentalism and the American Polity," in *The Fundamentalism Phenomenon*, ed. Norman J. Cohen (Grand Rapids, Mich.: Eerdmans, 1990), chapter 7.

27. Wuthnow, *Restructuring of American Religion*, chapter 9.

28. For a brief commentary on the conflict between Jerry Falwell's variety of fundamentalism and that of Jim and Tammy Bakker's PTL Club, see George M. Marsden, "Defining American Fundamentalism," in *Fundamentalist Phenomenon*, ed. Cohen, 27.

29. Hodding Carter III, "Like It or Not, Religion Has a Place in Politics," *Wall Street Journal*, 15 February 1990, A15.

30. For evidence that this shift is already under way, see D. Shribman, "Going Mainstream: Religious Right Drops High-Profile Tactics, Works on Local Level," *Wall Street Journal*, 26 September 1989, 1.

Chapter 3

ROBERT BOOTH FOWLER

1. For a succinct version, see Kenneth Wald, *Religion and Politics in the United States* (New York: St. Martin's Press, 1987), 187–89.

2. See, for example, the cover story, "Born-Again Politics," in *Newsweek*, 15 September 1980, l, 28–36.

3. Frances Fitzgerald, "A Disciplined, Charging Army," *The New Yorker* 57 (18 May 1981): 53–141.

4. For a good discussion of the culture-wars thesis, see Robert Wuthnow, *The Restructuring of American Religion* (Princeton: Princeton University Press, 1988).

5. See, for instance, John H. Simpson, "Moral Issues and Status Politics," in *The New Christian Right*, ed. Robert C. Liebman and Robert Wuthnow (New York: Aldine, 1984), chapter 10; Wald, *Religion and Politics*, chapter 7; Robert Booth Fowler, *Religion and Politics in America* (Methuchen, N.J.: Scarecrow, 1985), chapter 8.

6. See Lyman Kellstedt, "The Meaning and Measurement of Evangelicalism: Problems and Prospects," in *Religion and Political Behavior in the United States*, ed. Ted Jelen (New York: Praeger, 1989), 3–21; also see definitions used in Corwin Smidt, ed., *Contemporary Evangelical Political Involvement* (Lanham, Md.: University Press of America, 1989).

7. See, for instance, James Davison Hunter, *American Evangelicalism: Conservative Religion and the Quandary of Modernity* (New Brunswick, N.J.: Rutgers University Press, 1983).

8. Some examples of definition that are cultural in this sense may be found in: Nancy T. Ammerman, *Bible Believers: Fundamentalists in the Modern World* (New Brunswick, N.J.: Rutgers University Press, 1987); Randall Balmer, *Mine Eyes Have Seen the Glory: A Journey into the Evangelical Subculture in America* (New York: Oxford University Press, 1989); and A. G. Mojtabai, *Blessed Assurance: At Home with the Bomb in Amarillo, Texas* (Boston: Houghton, Mifflin, 1986).

9. George Marsden,"The Evangelical Denomination," in *Piety and Politics: Evangelicals and Fundamentalists Confront the World*, ed. Richard John Neuhaus and Michael Cromartie (Washington: Ethics and Public Policy Center, 1987), 57–68.

10. See the classic effort Peter Benson and Dorothy Williams, *Religion on Capitol Hill: Myths and Realities* (New York: Harper and Row, 1982).

11. See Clyde Wilcox, *God's Warriors: The Christian Right in Twentieth-Century America* (Baltimore: Johns Hopkins University Press, 1992); Anson Shupe and William Stacey, "The Moral Majority Constituency," Liebman and Wuthnow, eds., *New Christian Right* generally; Neuhaus and Cromartie, eds. *Piety and Politics*; and Clyde Wilcox, "The New Christian Right and the Mobilization of the Evangelicals," in *Religion and Political Behavior*, ed. Jelen 139–56.

12. See, for a good example, A. James Reichley, *Religion in American Public Life* (Washington: Brookings, 1985), 311–39.

13. See here such collections as Liebman and Wuthnow, eds., *New Christian Right*; or, Michael Lienesch, "The Paradoxical Politics of the Religious Right," *Soundings* 66 (Spring 1983); or, James L. Guth, "The Politics of the 'Evangelical Right': An Interpretive Essay" (Paper delivered at the American Political Science Convention, 1981). These are three interesting and different approaches in a large literature.

14. Wald, *Religion and Politics*, 190–91.

15. Richard John Neuhaus, "What the Fundamentalists Want," in *Piety and Politics*, ed. Neuhaus and Cromartie, 5–18.

16. On Falwell, see Jerry Falwell, *Listen, America* (Garden City, N.J.: Doubleday, 1980); Jerry Falwell, "An Agenda for the 1980s," in *Piety and Politics*, ed.

Neuhaus and Cromartie, 111–23; Hubert Morken, *Pat Robertson: Where He Stands* (Old Tappan, N.J.: Revell, 1988).

17. There is much on the Moral Majority. See Anson Shupe and William Stacey, "Moral Majority Constituency," in *New Christian Politics*, ed. David G. Bromley and Anson D. Shupe (Macon, Ga.: Mercer University Press, 1984); Liebman and Wuthnow, ed., *New Christian Right*; and other sources cited in specific footnotes. On interest groups in the area of religion and politics, including those of the NCR, see Allen Hertzke, *Representing God in Washington: The Role of Religious Lobbies in the American Polity* (Knoxville: University of Tennessee Press, 1988); and Fowler, *Religion and Politics*, chapters 7 and 8.

18. Allen Hertzke, "Faith and Access: Religious Constituencies and the Washington Elites," in *Religion and Political Behavior*, ed. Jelen, 259–74.

19. Matthew Moen, "Religion and the Congressional Agenda," *Extensions*, Spring 1985, 7–8; Hertzke, *Representing God*. For an earlier period, see Benson and Williams, *Religion on Capitol Hill*.

20. Jerome Himmelstein, *To The Right. The Transformation of American Conservatism* (Berkeley: University of California Press, 1990), chapter 4.

21. See Tod A. Booker, Lawrence W. Moreland, and Robert P. Steed. "Party Activists and the New Religious Right," in *Religion in American Politics*, ed. Charles W. Dunn (Washington: Congressional Quarterly Press, 1989), 161–75; Allen Hertzke, "Pat Robertson's Crusade and the GOP: A Strategic Analysis" (Paper delivered at the Midwest Political Science Convention, 1989); Corwin Smidt and James Penning, "A House Divided: A Comparison of Robertson and Bush Delegates to the 1988 Michigan Republican State Convention" (Paper delivered at the Midwestern Political Science Convention, 1988); and John C. Green and James L. Guth, "God and the GOP: Religion among Republican Activists," in *Religion and Political Behavior*, ed. Jelen, 223–41.

22. See, for instance, Corwin Smidt, "Evangelicals in Presidential Elections: A Look at the 1980s," *Election Politics* 5 (Spring 1988): 2–11; James L. Guth, "Political Converts: Partisan Realignment among Southern Baptist Ministers," *Election Politics* 3 (Winter 1985–1986): 2–6; and James L. Guth, "Southern Baptists and the New Right," in *Religion in American Politics*, ed. Jelen, 177–90.

23. And all this came before the real weakness of the late 1980s; Wald, *Religion and Politics*, chapter 7.

24. Wuthnow, *Restructuring of American Religion*.

25. Emmett Buell, Jr., "An Army that Meets Every Sunday? Popular Support for the Moral Majority in 1980" (Paper delivered at the American Political Science Convention, 1983); Jerry Perkins, "The Moral Majority as a Political Reference in the 1980 and 1984 Elections," in *Religion and Political Behavior*, ed. Jelen 157–68; Ronald Stockton, "The Falwell Core" (Paper delivered at the American Political Science Convention, 1985).

26. See Tina Rosenberg, "How the Media Made the Moral Majority," *Washington Monthly*, May 1982, 26–29, 32–34; William Martin, "The Birth of the Media Myth," *Atlantic Monthly*, June 1981; and Jeffrey K. Hadden, "Televangelism and Politics," in *Piety and Politics*, ed. Neuhaus and Cromartie, 390–94.

27. Wald, *Religion and Politics*, 205.

28. Most recently, Steve Bruce, *The Rise and Fall of the New Christian Right* (Oxford: Oxford University Press, 1988).

29. See Hubert Morken, "Religious Lobbying at the State Level: Case Studies

in a Continuing Role for the New Christian Right" (Paper delivered at the American Political Science Convention, 1990); see Paul Weyrich's evaluation in 1990, brought to my attention by Morken.

30. W. Craig Bledsoe, "Post-Moral Majority Politics: The Fundamentalist Impulse in 1988" (Paper delivered at the American Political Science Convention, 1990).

31. See Kim A. Lawton, "Lobbying for God," *Christianity Today*, 16 July 1990, 32–34.

32. Rebecca E. Klatch, *Women of the New Right* (Philadelphia: Temple University Press, 1987); Hertzke, "Pat Robertson's Crusade"; John C. Green and James L. Guth, "The Christian Right in the Republican Party: The Case of Pat Robertson's Supporters," *Journal of Politics* 50 (1988): 150–65; Lyman Kellstedt, "Evangelicals and Political Realignment" (Paper delivered at the American Political Science Convention, 1986); and Lyman Kellstedt, "Religion and Partisan Realignment" (Paper delivered at the Midwest Political Science Convention, 1989).

33. Lyman Kellstedt and Mark Noll, "Religion and Voting for President, and Party Ideology, 1948–1984," in *Religion and American Politics*, ed. Mark Noll (New York: Oxford University Press, 1990), chapter 16.

34. Jeffrey K. Hadden, "Televangelism and Politics," in *Piety and Politics*, ed. Neuhaus and Cromartie, 390–94.

35. I think Richard John Neuhaus and Allen Hertzke are both open to such a view. Both applaud the democratic, representational aspects of their appearance. See Neuhaus, "What the Fundamentalists Want"; and Hertzke, "Populist Echoes of Discontent: Jesse Jackson, Pat Robertson, and the Crucible of Liberal Culture" (Paper delivered at the American Political Science Convention, 1990).

36. For example, see James A. Speer, "The New Christian Right and Its Parent Company," in *New Christian Politics*, ed. Bromley and Shupe, 19–40.

37. See Wuthnow, *The Restructuring of American Religion*, for discussion of the culture-wars theme.

38. See, for example, Ronald Stockton, "The Evangelical Phenomenon: A Falwell-Graham Typology," in *Evangelical Political Involvement*, ed. Smidt, 45–74; Corwin Smidt, "Evangelicals versus Fundamentalists: An Analysis of the Political Characteristics and Importance of Two Major Religious Movements within American Politics" (Paper delivered at the American Political Science Convention, 1983); John Perkins, *A Call to Wholistic Ministry* (St. Louis: Open Door Press, 1980); Balmer, *Mine Eyes Have Seen*, chapter 7; and Robert Booth Fowler, *The New Engagement* (Grand Rapids: Eerdmans, 1982).

39. Falwell, "An Agenda for the 1980s."

40. Some useful readings: on the Bob Jones controversy, see *Moral Majority Report*, 14 July 1980, 4–7; on fundamentalist cultural attitudes, see Ammerman, *Bible Believers*; Ted G. Jelen, "The Effects of Religious Separatism on Partisan Ideology, Voting Behavior, and Issue Positions Among Evangelicals and Fundamentalists in the 1984 Elections" (Paper delivered at the American Political Science Convention, 1984); and Falwell, "An Agenda for the 1980s."

41. For example, see Mark Hatfield, *Between A Rock and a Hard Place* (Waco: Word Books, 1976), and Charles Colson, "The Lures and Limits of Political Power," in *Piety and Politics*, ed. Neuhaus and Cromartie, 173–85.

42. Marguerite Michaels, "Billy Graham: America Is Not God's Only Kingdom," *Parade Magazine*, 1 February 1981.

43. Some relevant citations: Stuart Rothenberg and Frank Newport, *The Evangelical Voter* (Washington: Institute for Government and Politics, 1984); Shupe and Stacey, "The Moral Majority Constituency"; James Guth, "Southern Baptists and the New Right." Contrast Ronald J. Sider, "An Evangelical Theory of Liberation," in *Piety and Politics*, ed. Neuhaus and Cromartie, 145–60, with Morken, *Pat Robertson*.

44. For three reflective examples, see Stephen Monsma, *Pursing Justice in a Sinful World* (Grand Rapids: Eerdmans, 1984); Mark A. Noll, Nathan O. Hatch, and George M. Marsden, *The Search for Christian America* (Westchester, Ill.: Crossway Books, 1983), chapter 6; James W. Skillen, "Can Politics Be Saved? What Must Evangelicals Do to Become Politically Responsible?" in *Evangelical Political Involvement*, ed. Smidt, 173–94.

45. See Morken, "Religious Lobbying at the State Level."

46. Hertzke quoted in Lawton, "Lobbying for God," 33.

47. A discussion of this topic should also include: Hertzke, "Faith and Access: Religious Constituencies and Washington Elites"; and, for my earlier assessment, Fowler, *Religion and Politics*, chapters 6 and 7.

48. For a moderate assessment, see Lawton, "Lobbying for God."

49. For example, see "Power, Glory—and Politics: Right-wing Preachers Dominate the Dial," *Time*, 17 February 1986, 62–68.

50. For an "official" view, see Randy Frame, "The State of Christian Broadcasting," *Christianity Today*, 20 March 1987, 48–50.

51. Wuthnow, *Restructuring of American Religion*, has his full argument here.

52. See the conception of American pluralism in Robert Bellah, Richard Madsen, William Sullivan, Ann Swidler, and Stephen Tipton, *Habits of the Heart: Individualism and Commitment in American Life* (Berkeley: University of California Press, 1985).

53. For a discussion of relevant cultural attitudes about religion and culture, see George Gallup, Jr., and Jim Castelli, *The People's Religion* (New York: Macmillan, 1989).

54. Hertzke, "Faith and Access"; see my *Religion and Politics in America* (Methuchen, N.J.: Scarecrow Press, 1985) for my argument that access was central.

55. Matthew Moen argues against my view in that he see the NCR as having great impact in Congress. But his work concentrates on the NCR in its early days and makes its case on agenda-setting as opposed to policy success. See *The Christian Right and Congress* (Tuscaloosa: University of Alabama Press, 1989).

56. For example, on the press, see S. Robert Lichter, Stanley Rothman, and Linda S. Lichter, *The Media Elite* (Bethesda, Md.: Adler and Adler, 1986); or, on the world of television and Hollywood, Ben Stein, *The View from Sunset Blvd.* (New York: Basic Books, 1979).

57. Rosenberg, "How the Media Made the Moral Majority."

58. See Buell, "An Army That Meets Every Sunday?"; Stockton, "The Falwell Core"; Wilcox, "The New Christian Right and the Mobilization of the Evangelicals"; and Wilcox, "The New Christian Right: Patterns of Political Beliefs."

59. See, for example, "Born Again at the Ballot Box," *Time*, 14 April 1980, 94; and "Power, Glory—and Politics," 62–68.

60. For his reading of "liberal" and the "reaction," see James Davison Hunter, "The Liberal Reaction," in *New Christian Right*, ed. Liebman and Wuthnow, 150–67.

61. In regard to *Christian Century*, see, for example, John Scanzoni, "Resurgent Fundamentalism," *Christian Century* 197 (10–17 September 1980): 847–49; Harvey Cox, "Fundamentalism as an Ideology," in *Piety and Politics*, ed. Neuhaus and Cromartie, 289–301; and Martin Marty, "Fundamentalism as a Social Phenomenon," in *Piety and Politics*, ed. Neuhaus and Cromartie, 305–20.

62. Neuhaus, "What the Fundamentalists Want," or Grant Wacker, "Searching for Norman Rockwell," in *Piety and Politics*, ed. Neuhaus and Cromartie, 329–53; or Kenneth D. Wald, Dennis E. Own, and Samuel S. Hill, Jr., "Habits of the Mind? The Problem of Authority in the New Christian Right," in *Religion and Political Behavior*, ed. Jelen, 93–103.

Chapter 4

CORWIN SMIDT

1. Michael Welch and David Leege, "Catholic Evangelicalism and Political Orientations: A Case of Transcended Group Boundaries and Distinctive Political Values" (Paper delivered at the annual meeting of the Society for the Scientific Study of Religion, Salt Lake City, October, 1989).

2. James Davison Hunter, *American Evangelicalism: Conservative Religion and the Quandary of Modernity* (New Brunswick, N.J.: Rutgers University Press, 1983), 139.

3. Generally speaking, it would appear that the relative size of the evangelical voting bloc would increase about 2–3 per cent (e.g., from 20 per cent to 22 per cent) as a proportion of the total white electorate if Catholics who exhibit evangelical characteristics are not excluded from evangelical ranks by definition; whereas the size of the evangelical voting bloc diminishes significantly (e.g., from 20 per cent to 13 per cent) if weekly church attendance is used as a criterion variable in defining evangelical respondents. See, Corwin Smidt and Paul Kellstedt, "Evangelicals in the Post-Reagan Era" (Paper delivered at the Citadel Symposium on Southern Politics, Charleston, March 1990). For a discussion of various analytical problems in the study of evangelicals, see Corwin Smidt and Lyman Kellstedt, "Evangelicals and Survey Research: Interpretative Problems and Substantive Findings," in *The Bible, Politics, and Democracy*, ed. Richard John Neuhaus (Grand Rapids: Eerdmans, 1987), 81–102, 130–167; Lyman Kellstedt, "The Meaning and Measurement of Evangelicalism: Problems and Prospects," in *Religion and Political Behavior in the United States*, ed. Ted Jelen (New York: Praeger, 1989), 3–21; and Corwin Smidt, "Identifying Evangelical Respondents: An Analysis of 'Born-Again' and Bible Questions Used Across Different Surveys," in *Religion and Political Behavior*, ed. Jelen, 23–43. For a brief discussion of various analytical approaches to the study of evangelicals, see Corwin Smidt, "Evangelicals and the 1984 Election: Continuity or Change?" *American Politics Quarterly* 15 (1987): 419–44.

4. Roman Catholics who otherwise meet the "born-again" and "Bible" criteria are excluded from the ranks of evangelicals because their heritage is outside the evangelical camp and because their patterns of primary relationships are likely to be part of another religious subcommunity.

5. However, as will be discussed later in the paper, one particular survey employed a self-identification question in which respondents were simply asked to check on their surveys whether or not they were "Fundamentalist or Evangelical Christians."

6. The exception is when data from the CBS/*New York Times* National Election Exit Poll of 1988 are analyzed. There are several reasons why analysis is generally restricted to white respondents only. First, blacks who subscribe to evangelical tenets of the Christian faith are less likely to call themselves evangelicals than whites who so subscribe. See Ken Sidey, "What's a Word?" *Christianity Today* 34, no. 3 (5 February 1990): 40–41; and Ted Jelen, Clyde Wilcox, and Corwin Smidt, "Biblical Literalism and Inerrancy: A Methodological Investigation," *Sociological Analysis* 51 (Fall 1990): 307–13. Second, because the religious subcultures of white and black evangelicals are likely to be different and because social interaction between white and black evangelicals is likely to be less frequent than between black evangelicals and non-evangelicals, white and black evangelicals should be analyzed separately. But, given the relatively small numbers within the resultant black evangelical and non-evangelical categories, meaningful comparisons cannot be made between the two black groups, and, as a result, analysis is generally restricted to a comparison of white evangelicals and non-evangelicals. In the case of the CBS/*New York Times* exit-poll data of 1988, however, over 11,500 respondents were surveyed. As a result, meaningful comparisons can be made between evangelicals and non-evangelicals for both white and black respondents. Consequently, when the exit-poll data are analyzed, the analysis will include comparisons for both racial groups.

7. It should be noted that every survey has a "margin of error." Thus, one must remember that a particular percentage reflects a mid-point in a range of percentages in which the "true" percentage within the population is likely to fall. For example, assume that a survey is constructed to have a margin of error of plus or minus 3 percentage points with a 95 per cent confidence interval. If that survey then reveals that 23 per cent of the population are evangelicals, the proper interpretation is that one can be 95 per cent confident that the "true" percentage of evangelicals within the population falls somewhere between plus or minus 3 percentage points of 23 per cent (i.e., somewhere between 20 and 26 per cent of the population). Now assume that the next survey with a margin of error of plus or minus 4 percentage points reveals that 25 per cent of the population are evangelicals (i.e., somewhere between 21 and 29 per cent of the population). Has there been a "true" increase in the percentage of evangelicals over time? Given that there are margins of error associated with each survey, it becomes problematic to interpret whether such a marginal change over time reflects true change in the percentage of evangelicals or reflects the fact that the results of the later survey fall within the particular percentage range within which evangelicals are likely to be found.

8. These surveys include: the Gallup Poll of 27–30 August 1976, the Gallup Poll of 12 August 1980, the Gallup Poll of 13–16 May 1983, the Gallup Poll of 9–12 November 1984, the *Los Angeles Times* Poll of 8–14 July 1986, the *Los Angeles Times* Poll of 14–19 August 1987, and the General Social Survey of March 1988 conducted by the National Opinion Research Center at the University of Chicago.

9. For an analysis of the justification for this particular measurement approach, see Smidt, "Identifying Evangelical Respondents," 23–43.

10. In the 1988 survey, the "born-again" question was changed simply to "Do you consider yourself a born-again Christian?"

11. One advantage, given the constraints of surveys (e.g., the length of the survey, the patience of respondents), is that a single question, rather than a series of questions, can be used to identify evangelical respondents, thereby allowing the analyst to include several other questions within the survey. One disadvantage is that some respondents, while exhibiting the general characteristics of evangelicals (e.g., high view of Scripture and a born-again experience) either may not recognize the label or may not wish to be so identified, and, as a result, fail to classify themselves as such.

12. Prior to 1986, Gallup employed a three-prong measure to identify evangelical respondents. Subsequently, Gallup has generally employed a single question: "Do you consider yourself to be a born-again or evangelical Christian?"

13. These figures are based on the more conservative estimates of evangelicals found within the CPS studies. Steven Bruce emphasizes the growth in the prominence of the South as one component contributing to the rise of the New Christian Right. See Steven Bruce, *The Rise and Fall of the New Christian Right: Conservative Protestant Politics in America 1978–1988* (New York: Oxford University Press, 1988), 49.

14. Robert Wuthnow, "The Political Rebirth of American Evangelicals," in *The New Christian Right*, ed. Robert Liebman and Robert Wuthnow (New York: Aldine, 1983), 167–68.

15. See the discussion in Liebman and Wuthnow, eds., *New Christian Right* (New York: Aldine, 1983).

16. Clyde Wilcox, "Evangelicals and Fundamentalists in the New Christian Right: Religious Difference in the Ohio Moral Majority," *Journal for the Scientific Study of Religion* 25 (1986): 355–63; Corwin Smidt, "Evangelicals within Contemporary American Politics: Differentiating between Fundamentalist and Non-fundamentalist Evangelicals," *The Western Political Quarterly* 41 (1988): 601–20.

17. These data are reported in Corwin Smidt, " 'Born-Again' Politics: The Political Behavior of Evangelical Christians in the South and Non-South," in *Religion and Politics in the South: Mass and Elite Perspectives*, ed. Tod Baker, Robert Steed, and Laurence Moreland (New York: Praeger, 1983), 27–56.

18. Lyman Kellstedt, "Evangelicals and Political Realignment," in *Contemporary Evangelical Political Involvement: An Analysis and Assessment*, ed. Corwin Smidt (Lanham, Md.: University Press of America, 1989), 99–117.

19. Gallup's *Christianity Today* survey conducted in 1979 also revealed that evangelicals were, as a whole, more Democratic than Republican in their partisan identifications. See Hunter's analysis of the *CT* data in his book *American Evangelicalism*, 55–56.

20. Corwin Smidt, "The Partisanship of American Evangelicals: Changing Patterns over the Past Decade" (Paper delivered at the annual meeting of the Society for the Scientific Study of Religion, Washington, D.C., 1986).

21. This drop in Republican identification appears to have been related to the Iran-Contra affair. Surveys conducted by Richard Wirthlin for the White House revealed that the Republicans trailed the Democrats by 7 percentage points in late 1987, when those independents who said that they "leaned toward" one party were counted as partisans. See John White, *The New Politics of Old Values* (Hanover, N.H.: University Press of New England, 1988), 87.

22. For several exceptions, see Clyde Wilcox, "The New Christian Right and the Mobilization of the Evangelicals," in *Religion and Political Behavior*, ed. Jelen, 139–56; Corwin Smidt, "Evangelicals and the New Christian Right: Coherence versus Diversity in the Issue Stands of Evangelicals," in *Contemporary Evangelical Political Involvement*, ed. Smidt, 75–97; and, Lyman Kellstedt, "The Falwell Issue Agenda: Sources of Support among White Protestant Evangelicals," in *An Annual in the Sociology of Religion*, ed. Monty Lynn and David Moberg (New York: JAI Press, 1988). For a broader analysis, see Jerome Himmelstein, *To The Right: The Transformation of American Conservatism* (Berkeley: University of California Press, 1990).

23. The 1988 question differed somewhat from the 1980 and 1984 items in that the phrase "such as the Moral Majority" was dropped in 1988.

24. Emmett Buell and Lee Sigelman, "An Army That Meets Every Sunday? Popular Support for the Moral Majority, 1988," *Social Science Quarterly* 66 (1985): 426–34; Clyde Wilcox, "Popular Support for the Moral Majority in 1980: A Second Look," *Social Science Quarterly* 68 (1987): 157–66.

25. John H. Simpson, "Moral Issues and Status Politics," in *New Christian Right*, ed. Liebman and Wuthnow, 188–207. There is also evidence to suggest that a significant portion of the opposition to the Moral Majority was tied to the methods, rather than the goals, of the organization. See Joseph Tamney and Stephen Johnson, "Explaining Support for the Moral Majority," *Sociological Forum* 3 (1988): 234–55.

26. Jerry Perkins, "The Moral Majority as a Political Reference in the 1980 and 1984 Elections," in *Religion and Political Behavior*, ed. Jelen, 157–68.

27. Ibid., 162–64.

28. At least four different factors might be posited to account for this drop in ratings. One factor might be the absence of the Moral Majority as a reference frame for the question in 1988; this factor, of course, assumes the Moral Majority was a group that gave a somewhat more positive embodiment to the phrase "evangelical groups active in politics." A second factor may be that the decline is tied, in part, to the PTL/Swaggart scandals, while a third factor might be that the drop is somehow associated with the impact of the Robertson campaign. A final factor may that the American voters, evangelicals included, were upset with the particular rhetoric or means by which "evangelical groups" attempted to get their social legislation passed during Reagan's second term.

29. For a discussion of some of the tensions exacerbated by the presence of members of the Christian Right within the Republican Party, see John Green and James Guth, "The Christian Right in the Republican Party: The Case of Pat Robertson's Supporters," *Journal of Politics* 50 (1988): 150–65.

30. Some analysts have argued that, given the presence of positivity biases in the thermometer scores, some adjustments in reported scores are necessary. As a result, some scholars have classified only those individuals as supporters of the Religious Right who assign a thermometer score to the "evangelical groups . . ." item at least 10 degrees warmer than their mean thermometer rating for all other groups in the survey. While there may be some merit to adjusting scores, this would be a more important consideration when the particular group being analyzed is highly evaluated in the first place, but such is not been the case with the "evangelical groups . . ." item. Moreover, a 10-degree difference is a fairly arbitrary criterion; why 10 degrees as opposed to 5 or 15 degrees? Finally, this

approach does not take into account the absolute nature of the scores, only their relative nature. Hypothetically, therefore, any respondent who gave a score of zero to all other groups in the survey, but gave a score of 10 to the "evangelical groups . . ." item would, thereby, be classified as a supporter of the New Religious Right. For the sake of simplicity, therefore, I have used just reported scores at their "face value." The subsequent analysis of the social and political characteristics of supporters of the New Religious Right seems to confirm much of what would have been expected impressionistically. Consequently, it is doubtful that this procedure has distorted greatly, if at all, the subsequent findings related to the supporters of the New Religious Right.

31. This classification scheme draws upon that used by Wilcox. See Wilcox, "New Christian Right," 139–56.

32. Several of the explanations are discussed in Ted Jelen and Clyde Wilcox, "The Effects of Religious Self-Identifications on Support for the New Christian Right: An Analysis of Political Activists" (Paper delivered at the annual meeting of the Society for the Scientific Study of Religion, Virginia Beach, November, 1990).

33. Clyde Wilcox, "Political Action Committees of the New Christian Right: A Longitudinal Analysis," *Journal for the Scientific Study of Religion* 27 (1988): 60–71.

34. Matthew Moen, *The Christian Right and Congress* (Tuscaloosa: University of Alabama Press, 1989).

35. By using adjusted thermometer-score ratings as described in footnote 30 above and by classifying as evangelicals those Catholics who shared evangelical theological beliefs, Wilcox found that slightly more than one-third of the white evangelicals could be classified as supporters of the New Christian Right in 1980.

36. See, for example, the discussion in Wilcox, "New Christian Right."

37. Based on the numbers falling within each issue group in Wilcox's analysis, it would appear that about 60 per cent of the evangelical community could be potentially attracted to the New Religious Right, whereas the issue positions of the remaining 40 per cent likely would put them outside any potential appeal on the part of the New Religious Right. See Wilcox, "New Christian Right."

38. Thomas C. Atwood, "Through a Glass Darkly: Is the Christian Right Overconfident It Knows God's Will?" *Policy Review* 54 (Fall 1990): 46.

39. Corwin Smidt and James M. Penning, "Religious Self-Identifications and Support for Robertson: An Analysis of Delegates to the 1988 Michigan Republican State Convention," *Review of Religious Research* 32 (1991); Jelen and Wilcox, "Effects of Religious Self-Identifications." Steven Bruce has also argued that, while organizations of the New Religious Right may be able to command sufficient resources to have certain issues placed on the political agenda, they appear to lack the ability to form stable, effective coalitions. See Bruce, *Rise and Fall.*

40. Atwood, "Through a Glass Darkly."

41. Brent Staples, "Black Conservatives Get Little Respect," *Grand Rapids Press*, 2 January 1991.

42. See, for example, George Gallup, Jr., ed., *Public Opinion 1980* (Wilmington, Del.: Scholarly Sources, 1981), 188–89. However, this pattern is true only when "doctrinal" measures are used to identify evangelicals, i.e., holding a belief in biblical inerrancy that is coupled with attesting to a born-again experience and witnessing about one's faith. When a self-identification question is employed, blacks are less likely than whites to claim to be evangelicals. See footnote 6 above.

43. The question asked of respondents was whether a variety of characteristics applied to the respondent, e.g., married, gun-owner, Vietnam-era veteran. Among the various characteristics was the following: "fundamentalist or evangelical Christian." It should be noted that only Protestants who labeled themselves accordingly were subsequently classified as evangelicals in this paper. Several factors contributed to the lower percentage of evangelicals found through this self-classification measure than through the measurement questions used earlier in the paper (i.e., the religious affiliation, Bible, and born-again questions). While a lack of familiarity with the term "evangelical" and/or a desire not be identified as such might contribute to this lower estimate, a more likely factor relates to the use of the term "fundamentalist" before the term "evangelical." The term "fundamentalist" tends to have a more negative social connotation than the term "evangelical."

44. Though these particular issues were identified as the most important issues of the campaign regardless of the race or ideological orientation of the respondents, the similarity in the salience of these issues reveals nothing about the policy direction such respondents would take on these issues.

45. See, too, A. James Reichley, "Pietist Politics," in *The Fundamentalist Phenomenon*, ed. Norman Cohen (Grand Rapids: Eerdmans, 1990), 73–98.

46. The exception to this assertion would be in terms of any activities that are viewed by the press as threatening or encroaching upon First Amendment rights, particularly freedom of speech and freedom of the press. As a result, considerable press attention was given recently to the cases related to Two Live Crew and the Mapplethorpe exhibition at the Museum of Contemporary Art in Cincinnati.

47. Atwood, "Through a Glass Darkly," 46.

48. See, for example, Don Lattin, " 'God's Green Beret' Plans to Assault S.F. Demons," *San Francisco Chronicle*, 1 September 1990.

JAMES L. GUTH

1. My use of this term is very similar to that of Joseph Tamney and Stephen Johnson, "Church-State Relations in the Eighties," *Sociological Analysis* 48 (1987): 1–16.

2. A good overview of religious politics in Europe is Suzanne Berger, ed., *Religion in Western European Politics* (London: Frank Cass, 1982).

3. Louis Hartz, ed., *The Founding of New Societies* (New York: Harcourt Brace, 1964).

4. The literature on ethno-cultural history is now voluminous. For an early but still useful assessment, see Richard L. McCormick, "Ethno-Cultural Interpretations of Nineteenth-Century American Voting Behavior," *Political Science Quarterly* 89 (1974): 351–77.

5. Robert Wuthnow, *The Restructuring of American Religion* (Princeton: Princeton University Press, 1988); and Wade Clark Roof and William McKinney, *American Mainline Religion* (New Brunswick, N.J.: Rutgers University Press, 1987).

6. The classic studies of clerical politics are Jeffrey Hadden, *The Gathering Storm in the Churches* (New York: Doubleday, 1969), and Harold Quinley, *The Prophetic Clergy* (New York: Wiley, 1974). For a comprehensive recent study of Protestant clergy, see James L. Guth, John C. Green, Corwin Smidt, and Margaret

Poloma, "Pulpits and Politics: Protestant Clergy in the 1988 Elections," in *The Bible and the Ballot Box*, ed. James L. Guth and John C. Green (Boulder, Col.: Westview, 1991), chapter 5.

7. For a fascinating theological and political portrait of the Catholic bishops, see Richard Gelm, "The National Conference of Catholic Bishops" (Paper delivered at the annual meeting of American Political Science Association, San Fransisco, 30 August–2 September 1990).

8. Michael Welch, David Leege, and Lyman Kellstedt, "Pastoral Cues and Congregational Response" (Paper delivered at the annual meeting of the American Political Science Association, San Francisco, 30 August–2 September 1990).

9. See, for example, James L. Guth and John C. Green, "Politics in a New Key: Religiosity and Participation Among Political Activists," *Western Political Quarterly* 42 (1990): 153–79; and John C. Green, James L. Guth, and Cleveland Fraser, "Religion and Presidential Campaign Contributors," in *The Bible and the Ballot Box*, ed. Guth and Green, chapter 7.

10. For the most recent evidence on evangelical voters, mainline Protestants, black Protestants, and Catholics, see the chapters by Corwin Smidt, Lyman Kellstedt, Paul Kellstedt, Clyde Wilcox, Henry Kenski, and William Lockwood in *The Bible and the Ballot Box*, ed. Guth and Green.

11. "Portrait of the Super Tuesday Voters," *New York Times*, 10 March 1988; and "Portrait of the Voters," *New York Times*, 8 November 1990.

12. Byron E. Shafer, "The New Cultural Politics," *PS* 28 (1985): 221–31; "The People, The Press and Politics: Post-Election Typology Survey" (Unpublished report), *Times Mirror*, November 1988; and "The People, the Press, and Politics, 1990" (Unpublished report), *Times Mirror*, 19 September 1990.

Index of Names